UNDERSTANDING
RANDALL KENAN

UNDERSTANDING CONTEMPORARY AMERICAN LITERATURE

Matthew J. Bruccoli, Founding Editor

Linda Wagner-Martin, Series Editor

UNDERSTANDING

# RANDALL KENAN

James A. Crank

THE UNIVERSITY OF
SOUTH CAROLINA PRESS

Cloth and ebook editions published by the University of South Carolina Press, 2019
Paperback edition published in Columbia, South Carolina,
by the University of South Carolina Press, 2021

www.uscpress.com

Manufactured in the United States of America

30 29 28 27 26 25 24 23 22 21
10 9 8 7 6 5 4 3 2 1

Library of Congress Cataloging-in-Publication data
can be found at http://catalog.loc.gov/.

ISBN 978-1-61117-958-3 (cloth)
ISBN 978-1-61117-959-0 (ebook)
ISBN 978-1-64336-188-8 (paperback)

For Trudier Harris,
my teacher,
my mentor,
my colleague,
my friend.

# CONTENTS

# SERIES EDITOR'S PREFACE

The Understanding Contemporary American Literature series was founded by the estimable Matthew J. Bruccoli (1931–2008), who envisioned these volumes as guides or companions for students as well as good nonacademic readers, a legacy that will continue as new volumes are developed to fill in gaps among the nearly one hundred series volumes published to date and to embrace a host of new writers only now making their marks on our literature.

As Professor Bruccoli explained in his preface to the volumes he edited, because much influential contemporary literature makes special demands, "the word *understanding* in the titles was chosen deliberately. Many willing readers lack an adequate understanding of how contemporary literature works; that is, of what the author is attempting to express and the means by which it is conveyed." Aimed at fostering this understanding of good literature and good writers, the criticism and analysis in the series provide instruction in how to read certain contemporary writers—explicating their material, language, structures, themes, and perspectives—and facilitate a more profitable experience of the works under discussion.

In the twenty-first century Professor Bruccoli's prescience gives us an avenue to publish expert critiques of significant contemporary American writing. The series continues to map the literary landscape and to provide both instruction and enjoyment. Future volumes will seek to introduce new voices alongside canonized favorites, to chronicle the changing literature of our times, and to remain, as Professor Bruccoli conceived, contemporary in the best sense of the word.

Linda Wagner-Martin, Series Editor

# PREFACE

## *Remembering Randall Kenan (1963–2020)*

It would be difficult, if not impossible, to overstate Randall Kenan's importance to American literature and culture. Randall was a critical bridge for understanding the complicated connections between African American and gay vernaculars; in the tradition of Baldwin and Du Bois, he was a preeminent voice articulating the mystery and magic of American Blackness; a passionate and stalwart advocate of preserving foodways, Randall celebrated the bounty and creativity of Southern and American cuisines; he found music in muscadine and poetry in persimmons; he wrote about the complex nuances that attend belonging to but feeling disconnected from your home, family, region, and nation; he was a storyteller of an invented land, at once profoundly mythic and also positively mundane, a world he inhabited with people whom he loved desperately and with abandon; he gave us characters as vibrant, vivid, and alive in his Tims Creek as they were in his homeland of Chinquapin, North Carolina; he was, in the words of Terry McMillan, "our black Garcia Marquez," a writer who seamlessly blended the spiritual world with the human; for Randall, all matters of the heart were as sacred as a church altar.

He was all of those things. But he was also a warm, funny, and deeply sensitive man who made family of his students, colleagues, mentors, and fellow authors. His laughter was infectious. He was deeply humble; he never spoke of his many successes or awards. He loved to give people nicknames to show them how dear they were to him—my mentor Linda Wagner Martin was "Funky Wagner," while I was his "dear little brother." He had an endless capacity for love and forgiveness. He was unfailingly patient and kind. His generosity to those working their way up through the academy and publishing

A portion of this piece initially appeared as part of the tribute for Randall on "The Project for the History of Black Writing" (http://www.projecthbw.ku.edu/obituaries/in-memoriam-randall-kenan/). My thanks to Maryemma Graham and the other editors of the site for permission to reprint.

was well-known, even though Randall rarely publicized it. His magic was his unceasing humanity.

He was my friend.

On August 28th, 2020, we lost him. I say "we" because, even though I felt the loss acutely, I know that Randall found his way into so many hearts across the world. For those of us who loved him, he was more than just his accomplishments, more than just a Guggenheim-winning, National Book Award finalist, and more than just his stories. For a gay teenager growing up in the South, *A Visitation of Spirits* was not just a novel, it was an opening to a way of belonging; Randall didn't just craft a beautiful story, he gave kids like me a genealogy to attach ourselves to, a critical perspective and proud visibility. And though we might have lost Randall, we will never lose that.

As a professor at the University of Alabama, I had been teaching Randall's books for years, and when I got the opportunity to write a monograph solely on his work, I was elated. When I began working on what would become *Understanding Randall Kenan,* I wondered whether Randall might agree to an interview for the final chapter of the book. He graciously agreed, and from our first conversation together, we found deep kinship. In my first interview with him, Randall talked about how crafting intimacies was at the heart of all his writing, especially intimacies that crossed over various axes of race, sexuality, and age. Randall found that ability to fully and freely share one's heart, even though it meant willfully crossing lines, shunning constructed divisions, and knowingly breaking the rules was at the foundation of who he was as an author and a person. He said, "I think it takes a certain kind of person who's willing to play like that. To extend themselves. And it's something of a dance, a metaphor for intimacy. That they're willing to dance with each other. And let go of a certain fear and not be so guarded. If you're too guarded, you won't be able to achieve that. And I see it happening, and it's a beautiful thing when it does. But it's rare when it happens."

Randall Kenan's work was a beautiful thing.

Randall Kenan's life was a rare gift.

At the end of that December day, Randall told me that he felt lucky because he had so many books to look to for guidance on what it means to be human, especially when he was young. He said, "I've been so fortunate, because I feel there are so many. I mean I'm a poor boy from Chinquapin, North Carolina; when I say I had a really good education, I don't mean I was Winston Churchill or anything. I wasn't studying Greek and Latin, but I was given some good books to read. Enough to last me the rest of my life." What blissful luck that we have Randall Kenan's books to help us understand the mystery and terror of being a human. They are enough to last us the rest of our lives.

I hope this book can be a solace and comfort to other friends and fans of Randall Kenan, an acknowledgment of the stunning and soulful contribution he made to literature and culture, to our understanding of what it means to be human in a specific place and time, to our happiness, to our determination to carry on and live and love. It's a remarkable thing his last collection asks us to imagine what magic there might be in growing two wings, to veil your face and feet—as Randall did in his very private life—but more importantly, to soar into the sky far above a world that has the power to wound you in ways that take years to acknowledge and heal. If there is any solace in Randall's passing it may be this: He taught us the secret language of magic, to walk on water, to speak to the dead, to fly. In my mind, I can see him now, a two-winged creature, all human angelic and free.

And he is flying high.

Tuscaloosa, AL
October 2020

# ACKNOWLEDGMENTS

First, I would very much like to thank Randall for his generosity and willingness to allow me to pepper him with questions, bug him with details, ask him to vet sources and facts, and, in general, poke and prod through the complexities of his fiction and life. I am especially grateful to him for allowing me to interview him twice: once for information concerning his biography and once for the interview that makes up the entirety of Appendix A. I am also thankful for the "Tims Creek Genealogy" that Mr. Kenan provided to me and that appears here as Appendix B; it will doubtless prove useful to scholars and readers of his fiction. It is, indeed, a rare thing to have an opportunity to meet one of your heroes but quite another thing entirely to have the experience be so affirming, such a sincere and genuine pleasure. Thank you so much, Randall.

Second, every book needs an entire separate thank-you entry for Linda Angell. I don't think I can thank her enough, not simply for the tireless work she does on my books but for just being who she is: a bestest friend, a confidant, a collaborator, and a world-class editor. Every writer should have his or her own Linda Angell—but you should find your own. I call dibs on mine.

Beyond those two fantastic folks, I have an entire village to thank for its emotional and intellectual support, but I should start first with the University of Alabama, and specifically both the College of Arts and Sciences and the Department of English, which have provided so much financial support and encouragement during this process, especially the CARSCA Grant Committee, who funded my trips to Chapel Hill to speak with Mr. Kenan twice. I have some of the best colleagues ever, and they have been there for me every step of this process, so thank you: Bob Olin, Tricia McElroy, Joel Brouwer, Wendy Rawlings, Trudier Harris, David Deutsch, and all my colleagues on Team English. Special thanks to Jim Denton at USC Press and to Linda Wagner-Martin always—a true friend and the best mentor any student could ever dream of having.

I have had wonderful friends and family (biological and chosen) who have helped me in more ways than I can say: Jeff (every book is yours); Phyllis and

Bill Agnew; Dad, Shelly, Steve, Don, and Daniel Crank; Abbie and Renee; Merinda, Nathan, Arlo; Memorie, Joe, Sam, Tucker; Samantha Hansen; Mark Hernandez, Cristian Asher, Dean Skiles; Heidi Norwood; Molly McGehee & FLOBEBE; Erich Nunn and Amy Clukey (the band); Michael Bibler and the whole SSSL crew; Kate, Layton, and Joshua Whitman; Sharon Holland; the best students any professor has ever had; my family of friends that I have been stuncle to; and always, of course, Maddie, forever and ever, amen.

And, finally, this book has benefited from amazing graduate students, who have worked with me to compile bibliographies, edit, and work through indices. Thank you so much: Candace Chambers, Jenna Lyles, Sarah Landry, Tucker Legerski, and Jeffrey Jones.

# CHAPTER 1

## Understanding Randall Kenan

> "I wanted to write before I knew I wanted to write, and write I did, talking back, writing back, on paper, to Beatrix Potter, to Robert Louis Stevenson and Edgar Allan Poe and Tom Swift and the Hardy Boys."
>
> Randall Kenan, "An Ahistorical Silliness" in *The Fire This Time*

Though Randall Garrett Kenan was born in the early spring of 1963 in Brooklyn, New York, he found himself very quickly the citizen of a state that would become not just his adopted homeland, but, indeed, the central focus of much of his intellectual and artistic exploration: North Carolina. Only six weeks old, the young Kenan was shuttled off from the big city of New York to the small, rural community of Duplin County, North Carolina, where he lived briefly with his grandfather and his seamstress grandmother in the thriving small town of Wallace. At first, his grandparents—who ran a dry-cleaning establishment—hired someone to take care of the boy while they worked, but his great-aunt, Mary Fleming, his grandfather's sister, and his great-uncle Redden immediately "took a shine"[1] to the baby and would take him away for weekends to the family farm in Chinquapin, "about fifteen miles east of Wallace," Kenan remembered; the farm and the country were very different from the town where Kenan's grandparents lived. It was, as he recalled later, "deep, deep country, on the edge of the Angola swamp, it lay on a dirt road, surrounded by fields and woods. My first memories of the place are apple trees, grapevines, pine trees, and an oak tree so large it could blot out the sun, with limbs as thick as small automobiles, a trunk of truly elephantine proportions."[2]

Mary quickly recognized that Kenan's grandparents were too involved in running their business to take care of an infant. "One weekend she just didn't bring me back,"[3] he recalled with a laugh, and "Old Field Road became my home."[4] In a short amount of time, Kenan began to call Mary "Mama." When Kenan was only three years old, Redden died unexpectedly. In his essay "Brother Rabbit versus Brother Fox," Kenan muses that the man's death is one of his earliest memories: "When I ask people about their earliest memory, it truly puzzles me when they say it's from preschool, or kindergarten or first grade. Perhaps they are being cautious, but I remember images vividly from ages two and three and, I believe, from earlier. But I have no doubt about three, for that is how old I was when my great-uncle Redden died on my quilt."[5]

The loss of Redden greatly affected Kenan's family. In the wake of the man's death, Kenan remembered his grandfather saying to his great-aunt, "You're here by yourself, so why don't you just keep the boy?" She did, and a young Randall Kenan remained with her for the rest of his childhood and adolescence.

Kenan's biological parents were not married, and the young boy never knew much of his mother, who stayed behind in Brooklyn. However, his father moved back to Wallace not too long after Kenan was adopted. Still, Kenan's intellectual, emotional, and familial mentor was Mary, who was adamant that the young boy learn the fundamentals of language from an early age; she taught him to read when he was only four years old. A kindergarten teacher by trade and used to working with children Kenan's age, Mary Fleming could relate well to the child in her care. She bought him books: one of his first loves. Kenan remembered that the first book she got him was "*Peter Cottontail,* and on my fifth Christmas I got this adaptation of *Moby Dick,* which I still can't find, because that book was kind of long gone, but I remember it vividly because it was one of those graphic adaptations for younger readers with big pictures and all that sort of thing."[6] The young Kenan found himself captivated by the world of words and images. "I was reading all the time," he recalled. "I discovered comic books not long after that. *The Swiss Family Robinson, Robinson Crusoe,* all those books that none of my students read anymore."

Kenan's childhood, though impoverished and rural, was rich in support, education, and love. He found himself—especially later in life—looking back on his early experiences with a great deal of fondness and appreciation. The farm was his emotional center, but the nearby town "bustl[ed] like a little beehive, sprung up around a railroad depot, a warren of small tobacco warehouses and poultry plants, several stone's throws from Wilmington."[7] And, of course, Kenan had the church: "Two churches in fact. First Baptist and St. Louis. Both Baptist . . . My mama was zealous about my going to church, and I remember too many sermons to be in my right mind, and the pastors Hestor, and Lassiter the younger, who succeeded Lassiter the senior. There were revivals in

September and Vacation Bible School in June, when the blueberry season came, and Sunday school each and every Sunday. . . . Church remained an indelible mark on my growing up, and, no matter how far or how fast I run, the lessons of Baptist Protestantism and southern Calvinism will be etched on my brain—probably my soul—the way circuits are hardwired to a motherboard."[8]

Kenan found a love for reading through the Bible, but he also discovered a passion for making up his own stories. His favorite subject in school was initially science, specifically physics. In high school, the young man had been in the Minority Introduction to Engineering program (MITE), which sought to introduce young, marginalized students to the concepts of engineering. Kenan recalled the program as part of a larger national ferment: "You know, in the late '70s, early '80s, they were much more aggressive and pronounced in outreach to young poor kids of color."[9] But even his interest in science was tinged with a connection to fiction and stories. "I think my initial fascination was with science fiction," Kenan admitted. "I mean that led me into [writing], and I actually remember my high school physics teacher was extremely discouraging [about reading science fiction stories]."

Though he voraciously devoured science textbooks and memorized equations, Kenan also found himself interested in his own capacity for storytelling. During high school, he wrote what he later labeled "several bad novels in longhand" that were dark and macabre, more Edgar Allan Poe than William Faulkner. "I still have some of those stories," he recalled. The stories would start out dark and mysterious and suddenly switch: "and then it would be Space Opera. You know, science fiction." These stories he found himself writing were a way of dealing with a gap the young writer had found between the world he saw and the worlds he read about: "Writing is an extension of reading, and I guess that, in many ways, I wanted to write the stories that I wasn't finding to read, that nobody was writing—that was a huge motivation, as well."

Though he knew he would always love Chinquapin and the farm, Kenan never considered staying in his hometown; remaining there never felt like a viable option to him. "There's nothing to do there," he remarked about Wallace. "I don't know what I would have done if I'd stayed. The only thing I could have done was teach school or become a farmer, and, you know, I wasn't interested in either one of those [professions]." Kenan's family also supported his decision to leave: "It was just assumed that you were going to go away, you know, when you grew up, that you would sort of go to college and then move on from there." He had decided to pursue a degree in physics in college because a friend of his who had gone to Georgia Tech convinced him that getting a bachelor's in physics before doing graduate work in engineering would work to his advantage in future employment. However, Kenan's family and town weren't so sure: "It was a very odd thing, especially in Dougal County, for a young black fella to actually want to do something like [go into the natural sciences], and people would look askance when I told them I'm going to go into physics," he remembered. But he persevered and decided to "learn all my equations and algorithms at Chapel Hill and then go on." Even despite his good planning, things didn't work out quite the way Kenan envisioned.

In the fall of 1981, Randall Kenan began a difficult freshman year at the University of North Carolina at Chapel Hill. He found himself confused about what direction to follow and not enjoying his science classes. After his first year, Kenan enrolled in a writing class with Max Steele, one of the preeminent professors of creative writing and an editor at *The Paris Review*. The young Kenan excitedly turned in his science fiction and mystery stories, but he was met with brutal rejection from his professor. "But I appreciated that sort of frankness," Kenan remembered. "[Steele] recommended that I start looking at people like Ellison and Baldwin," the latter of whom had been on Kenan's radar early in his life. As an avid reader of magazines like *JET* and a consumer of popular culture in general, Randall Kenan already was aware of the larger-than-life presence of James Baldwin. But he admitted, "I knew *about* Baldwin. I had not really read him that much." Really, the only memories Kenan had of Baldwin during his adolescence were of hearing his aunts talk about the writer's books, especially "the gay stuff." Kenan had a chance to meet Baldwin when the writer came to Chapel Hill during Kenan's senior year. The University frequently drew big name writers to campus—Alex Haley, John Irving, Nikki Giovanni—but it was Baldwin and Haley who made an impact on Kenan.

Kenan remembered James Baldwin sitting in on Professor Lee Greene's graduate seminar on African American literature; seeing the writer in person was almost too much for the precocious student to handle: "I was reading him, and I was reading interviews and stuff. I will never forget. I quoted something that he said on a Studs Terkel interview in like 1956 or something. He said, 'That was like twenty years ago, how the hell would I remember everything I say?'" Similarly, the novelist Alex Haley influenced Kenan's thoughts on writing as a profession and the difficulties involved in such a craft. "[Haley] was the first person who I remember talking about the idea of people who become writers have at some point spent a lot of their time alone which was . . . my childhood on a big farm out in the middle of a swamp, you know. And he talked about time on a ship, time in healing, and all that sort of thing. So, I'd been thinking about [writing during that time] increasingly."

It was also during Kenan's senior year at Chapel Hill that the young man began to work through a dramatic change in the style and subject of his writing. Part of the push to connect the pieces he'd been working on as an undergraduate was practical—Kenan was tasked with assembling a dossier of materials to graduate with honors. Ever precocious, the young writer graduated early and took courses with upperclassmen and honors students as a sophomore and a junior. His professors, from Louis D. Rubin to Doris Betts, encouraged his writing. At the time, Kenan found himself drawn particularly to fiction: "I was writing short stories, but I also started on a novel called *Ashes Don't Burn,* and that actually became *A Visitation of Spirits* in a sort of inverted way, but some of the stories I wrote wound up in *Let the Dead Bury Their Dead,* too."

During his time in Chapel Hill, Kenan had begun to form a community of other men who shared a similar celebration of their sexual identity. While not an ideal place for a queer-identified young man in the 1980s, the University of North Carolina was accepting enough of gay students and faculty: "There was a Carolina Gay Association, and those meetings were held in the Student Union, and you had local members. We had some local members, the faculty, not a whole lot. Probably the most famous being Gary Utz in the Department of Education." Though more "fringe" than mainstream, the small gay community of students in Chapel Hill found one another. Kenan remembered that finding his way into such a community was "very helpful": "I had openly gay friends before my senior year, but my senior year, me and my close friend moved into this house on Friendly Lane. The house was called The Castle. I had just turned twenty, and it had been founded twenty years ago. And for twenty years, it had nothing but gay men living in there. Everybody called it The Castle, but it was just a white clapboard house. The house is still there. It's fixed up much better than it was when we were there. It was kind of run down when we were there. They called it The Castle because queens lived there."

By the time he was ready to graduate, Randall Kenan had a pretty firm grip on who he was, but he still was not sure of exactly what he wanted to do. He had gone back and forth between wanting to write and wanting to work in the publishing field. But mostly he felt stuck.

His senior thesis professor, Doris Betts, became Kenan's friend and mentor. Unlike the somewhat pedantic Steele, Betts was appreciative of Kenan's areas of interest. At the time, Kenan recalled, he was "already getting very frustrated with social realism, and [Professor Steele] didn't seem to care. But Doris was very encouraging, and I think that was why I really started to write a lot like Latin American Boom writers who I was reading at the time." Those writers—figures like Julio Cortázar, Gabriel García Márquez, and Carlos Fuentes—were ones Max Steele didn't know but Doris did. "She was very encouraging in anything—well, not any experiment—but she was cool with experimentation. She was so well read and so intellectual," he recalled. Kenan decided to graduate a semester early; he had convinced himself that he belonged in the publishing world of New York City. At that time, he began to really "bug Doris to death [and she] wrote letters on my behalf to people she knew in New York. She wrote people at Harper & Row. That was the predecessor to HarperCollins. I went to a lot of places. I had a friend who lived in the Bronx, and I flew up there before I graduated and stayed with her and pounded the pavement for about two weeks."

Nothing really materialized from Kenan's hard work canvassing the publishing houses. He graduated from Chapel Hill in the fall of 1984 and promptly sank into a little bit of a depression. "After I graduated in December," Kenan recalled, "that January, I stayed with my grandfather for about a month and my great Aunt Eerie. I went to see her, and she had like sixteen children. And she's like, 'Boy, what you want to do?' and I said, 'I want to go and live in New York, to work in publishing.' And she said, 'Well, what's stopping you?' 'I don't know where to go.' Sort of sullen twenty-year-old, so she took down the phone, called one of her sons and said, 'This boy wants to come to New York, can he stay with you?'" His cousin answered the call, and soon, Randall Kenan was living in Newark, New Jersey; he followed many of the leads that he had established through his and Betts's letters. But his first potential job offer was an odd one—working for Jim Henson. "I was going to be a receptionist. It was back in the day when they still had receptionists," Kenan recalled. "I was going to be a receptionist, and I was also going to be making puppets, so I guess that was fun." But the young man worked for the Jim Henson Company for only one day before being offered a job at one of the most prestigious New York publishers, Random House.

Originally, Kenan got his job at Random House because the company had gotten into trouble with the Equal Opportunity Commission; the call had come down, Kenan remembered, "to increase their minority numbers, so what they said was, I'm hiring you as an office boy in waiting." During that time, Kenan found himself tasked with odd jobs: "I was a floater for about six months, and it was actually a great way to get to know such a big company. I would work for the accounts department. I'd go work in Random House publicity. I'd be the receptionist at Pantheon, and this and that and the other. And then an opening came up for the receptionist at Alfred A. Knopf, and that's how I wound up there . . . all because they had the band-aid to hire more black folk. So here I was a qualified black folk going to work for peanuts basically, and they made a position in-house temp until a full-time job came along. So, that's basically how I got my foot in the door."

By February 1985, Kenan had secured a job as a floater at Knopf; in that role, the young man found ample opportunities to read and study his craft.

Most of the work he did involved waiting around to be called or answering phones for administrators. In between those calls, he would read and plan the structures for his fictional universes. He fancied himself not just a novelist or fiction writer but a man of letters, "like George Bernard Shaw; in fact, one of the people that Doris sent me to was Rocky Mussolini, who I got to know later, fairly well, and he had actually done that. He'd written a novel. He'd written a collection of short stories, but his reputation was based on play writing. And he said pick one, stick with it, and eventually if you want to do something else on the side, fine, but get over this silly idea you have that you're going to do it all, because you're not."

Even though he was dissuaded from writing drama, the young Kenan went to the theater religiously. The off-Broadway scene in New York in the mid-1980s astonished him, and ticket prices were cheap enough to match his meager budget as a floater. "I got to see all of August Wilson's twenty on Broadway, including *Gem of the Ocean, Seven Guitars, Ma Rainey's Black Bottom,* that was playing when I first got to New York. And James Earl Jones in the first [production of] *Fences.*" Kenan was in New York City at the right time for the explosion of the Public Theater, too, "and that was much more affordable," he remembered. "But also Papp did nontraditional casting. I saw Denzel Washington do Richard III." While he was seeing plays in the evening, Kenan was reading and discovering up-and-coming writers, including a young Cormac McCarthy. He had the good fortune to learn from those in publishing, "people in the know" who had access to the best up-and-coming talent. Though McCarthy was not yet a best-selling writer, everyone Kenan knew was talking about him: "I mean *Blood Meridian* sold like eight hundred copies, but I was reading him on the PATH train, on the subways, back and forth from Newark."

Only two months after securing a job as a receptionist, Kenan moved into a position as assistant to the executive vice president at Alfred A. Knopf, a move that, "for me felt like my graduate school," he recalled. He stayed as assistant to the vice president for five years; in this capacity, he helped to edit dozens of books and honed his own craft in the process. More important, the job at Knopf gave Kenan a crucial window into the complicated process of publishing a novel. That world had opened to him in a way that it wouldn't to other authors his age. Back in Manhattan in the late 1980s, Kenan was surrounded by writers who were trying to make a living doing what they loved. "There was this series of apartments on West End Avenue that all these Ivy Leaguers sort of held, and it was sort of like a revolving door," Kenan recalled of that time. "You graduated from college and you moved in with one of these people; it was sort of like a network, but these were all Brown and Princeton folks. And here I was this little North Carolina Tar Heel southern man. But Rick Moody had lived in that apartment. And David Leavitt wrote *The Lost Language of Cranes* in my bed in the room I stayed." By 1988, Kenan had finished final revisions on what he hoped would be his first published novel, *A Visitation of Spirits.*

Kenan's memory of writing his debut novel is that it was written in a solitary space, a spot of silence he needed to write freely: "One of the reasons I wanted to leave my cousin's house in Newark was to have more space to write. It was while I was there that I could see *Visitation.* The book I was working on before, *Ashes Don't Burn,* was involved with lycanthropy and an older character, and so, I decided to pretty much invert it and make it a younger person in the same town that I was writing about, and a few other decisions came."

But *Visitation* was by no means composed solely during those four years in the late 1980s. "I was jumping right into writing as soon as I left college," Kenan said. "Doris [Betts] was pretty much—if you don't become a self-starter and write without me here asking you to turn stuff in at the end of a week, you're never going to do it. That's the kind of advice I give my students, too." Being around so many young, emerging writers was also useful for Kenan as he revised and edited *Visitation:* "Don Anthem was one of my early readers. He was sort of hanging out, working in and out of publishing, and Amy Holmes became my key reader." At twenty-five years old, Kenan had secret-insider advice as to what could make or break a debut novel. He knew how to approach editors, whom to talk to, and what to ask for, and he also knew that Grove Press was the ideal house to publish his work: "Grove was just so cool. Beckett and Genet and all those writers I admired. In fact, I just felt like a hip cat." Thinking back, Kenan admitted, "I was probably a real jerk to my editor because I was about twenty-five and thought I knew everything. I wouldn't want to deal with me back then."

Kenan quickly found himself overwhelmed by the response to his novel. In no time, all the people involved in publishing *A Visitation of Spirits* found that they had to reexamine their low expectations for a first-time novel. Kenan remembered, "I'll never forget one of my mentors, astronomical woman, she was the vice president in charge of advertising. When, in those days, most publishers would sell the paperback rights within the company and, with *A Visitation of Spirits,* Grove sold the paperback rights to Anchor Press for $7,500—not bad as my advance for the novel. They sold the paperback rights for $25,000, and I was just gleeful. I started making $13,500 a year; that was my take-home salary. I was making $18,000 at that point, so selling the paperback rights for anything over $20,000 was like, God! And I remember the VP of advertising said, 'Oh no, your first novel should be a disaster. That's horrible.'"

Even though he had a new novel coming out, Kenan found himself working all the time: "I was putting in thirty-hour weeks, coming in on weekends, that sort of thing. And being a writer and an editor is something that very few people do very well—at all." Fortunately, having an acclaimed novel in press allowed Kenan the flexibility to switch out of the grind of the publishing world to a profession that allowed a young writer time to work more productively: teaching.

After the publication of *Visitation,* Kenan worked part-time as a teacher for three universities and colleges—"until you get tenure, you're a scholar gypsy, or a gypsy scholar," he remembered. "I was only teaching at Sarah Lawrence one day a week and likewise at Columbia, one day a week. I wasn't making a princely sum, but I could pay my rent with a roommate. And then, at one point, I was teaching at Vassar, too, so I would be doing three classes at once which would sort of help out." Working as a professor was liberating for Kenan, but he found it to be a big change. "I had found this rhythm at work. I didn't have much of a social life, but I remember reading all the time. V. S. Naipaul led me to nonfiction, and he talks about when he first got out of Cambridge how he worked for the BBC. How he would come and do his stories for them and then he'd go out and have a light supper. Then he'd come back to that same typewriter and work on his own stuff. And that just sort of unified discipline appealed to me. And so, a lot of [my stories from that time] I started before I left Knopf, and I would do that thing because I had written *Visitation of Spirits* that way."

Though Kenan resented his teaching gig at first ("I wasn't much older than my students," he remembered years later), it did allow him a flexibility that was crucial to his writing schedule. While he was teaching during the day, Kenan would work at night, and the collection he found himself coming back to was a short story cycle that he would eventually title *Let the Dead Bury Their Dead*.

Though Kenan was excited about the new collection, he was understandably anxious about following up *Visitation* with a book that might not match its success. "I finished *Visitation of Spirits* in 1988, and I thought, 'Oh God, I need to do another book right away!'" he recalled. "So, I started on these stories, and a lot of these early stories began while I was still working in publishing with that same old, you know, work on their stuff during the day and my stuff at night." Initially, the stories that made up his new manuscript were part of his first novel: "Originally, *Visitation* was composed of four parts, and the fourth part just seemed unwieldy. So, then I sort of took it out and made it into *Let the Dead Bury Their Dead*. That novella was originally planned to be a part of *A Visitation of Spirits*." Even though the book got published in 1992 as a short-story cycle, Kenan "had always thought of it as a collection unified by the place of Tims Creek."

Though fictional, Tims Creek clearly became a stand-in for Duplin County and Chinquapin. Kenan explained that his desire to invent his own little world came, in large part, from the writers he had read growing up. "Well, all of the writers I admired most had [made up their own area]; Faulkner, of course. It just made a lot of sense to have your own little postage stamp that you could reinvent whenever you wanted to, manipulate any way you wanted to. It appealed to me." *Let the Dead Bury Their Dead* explored disparate characters and stories, all tethered to the central setting of Tims Creek. Kenan's model was a "sort of formal novel of stories. I had been thinking of something like Welty's book *The Golden Apples.* And so, the possibility for the short story, plus, you know, Doris Betts was my teacher, so I was very much interested in the short story and the form." *Let the Dead Bury Their Dead* was published by Harcourt Brace Jovanovich, and Kenan's editor there was a familiar friend from Chapel Hill, Elaine Mason. "She came to New York, and she went to work for Simon & Schuster. We stayed in touch, and she became a reader. She was very encouraging of me, and when I had the manuscript for the stories, we sent it to her," Kenan recalled.

At the time, Kenan was thinking long-term about his publishing deals. His agent encouraged him to negotiate a two-book deal that would send the stories in *Let the Dead Bury Their Dead* along with the idea of a nonfiction manuscript addressing blackness in America (which would eventually become *Walking on Water*). "He [my agent] was going to sell them together from one place, but Elaine didn't want the nonfiction. Anchor was going to do it, but then Knopf called and made an offer for the nonfiction; I got more money selling them separately than doing them together so that's how I wound up at Harcourt and at Knopf," he explained. Randall Kenan found himself able to negotiate more because *Let the Dead Bury Their Dead* became a huge success. Shortly after its publication, the collection was nominated for the *Los Angeles Times* Book Award for Fiction. More important, *Let the Dead Bury Their Dead* was a finalist for the National Book Critics Circle Award. Suddenly, Kenan found himself on the radar of a lot of readers for the first time. His acclaim allowed him more opportunities to focus on his work. "I kept doing more teaching and being asked to come read in places and getting grants," Kenan recalled of the time between 1992 and 1993. "I think that was one of the things that sustained me for a long time was I could get a Guggenheim and all of these things. That was really nice."

Awards and fellowships began to flow in, among them a Guggenheim, the Whiting Award, and the Sherwood Anderson Award, as well as the Rome Prize from the American Academy of Arts and Letters. New financial support allowed Kenan both to do the fieldwork for the nonfiction book he was dreaming of and to spend some time compiling that manuscript in Italy. His completed book, *Walking on Water,* became a four-year obsession for Kenan. In many ways, what spurred his interest in thinking broadly about issues of race and region in America was Naipaul: "he sort of became the model of my adult living anyway, and I just liked the way he would write fiction and nonfiction. I was at Knopf when he did *A Turn in the South.* So, I was really sort of just steeped in Naipaul. When he turned in a manuscript for *A Turn in the South,* my editor came and brought it to me and said, 'You're a southerner; can't you tell this better?' That book [*Turn*] actually gave me the chutzpah to try do *Walking on Water,* because I thought, 'Well I can do this, too.' I mean that was the idea. I hope I pulled it off."

Kenan returned from his writing time in Rome with a completed manuscript; he started a position in 1998 as the John Grisham Writer in Residence at the University of Mississippi in Oxford. Kenan was the fifth writer to serve the term (in the company of such luminaries as T. R. Pearson, Tim Gautreaux, and Mary Hood). Teaching in the Deep South was a different kind of challenge for Kenan, who found his students somewhat different from those he was used to at Columbia and Sarah Lawrence: "they were much more down-to-earth people. I mean I had people who'd been ex-military . . . some sorority sisters and that sort of thing too, but I had more, you know, not just sort of well-toned producers' kids from L.A."

Shortly after his year-long stay in Oxford, Mississippi (the first term served by a Grisham Writer in Residence for a full academic year) in 1999, Kenan moved to Memphis, Tennessee, where he took a job as an assistant professor of creative writing at the University of Memphis. *Walking on Water* was published that year and signaled a new turn for Kenan. Once an author of fantastical fiction—a kind of southern magical realist with a penchant for detail—Kenan was now one of the leading voices on issues of race and American identity. His new job was perfect for the writer because "that was the first time I had taught nonfiction, and they needed a nonfiction teacher, especially in that MFA program. So, that was my primary focus, and I would teach fiction to undergrads and then . . . I taught some fiction to graduate students too, but I focused a lot on nonfiction." He would stay in that position for four years; Kenan found himself growing fond of the Delta, and especially the excitement of Memphis in the early 2000s: "I got to see when they had just finished the [Redbirds] ballpark, and they were making a concerted effort to grow downtown. I lived in the Clarence House, and I loved it. I loved Memphis. I loved that whole river-town ethos, and they had just enough going on to make it fun. And downtown was,

I mean a lot of people who lived out in East Jesus, they thought downtown was still dangerous and they wouldn't come. You know, they would come down to Beale Street on the weekends. But other than that, it was still pretty off limits for a lot of people who lived out in Germantown and the like. Now that has changed dramatically."

For Kenan, "the teaching experience [in Memphis] was probably my favorite" because he got to engage in the classroom with a different kind of student, one who was not necessarily used to the privileges afforded to those at Ivy League schools like Columbia: "These were people who worked for FedEx, some were ex-military, some had full-time jobs. In the MFA program the students weren't getting into high-flying schools, but they could write. And I actually felt I had something to teach them. That was a really great experience," he remembered. However, after four years in the Mississippi Delta, the siren call of his home state became too much to resist.

During the course of his professional life, Randall Kenan has never strayed too far from North Carolina. He still has family in Duplin County, of course, and he has always found ways to get back to his alma mater in Chapel Hill. "Ten years after I had graduated, I did a year back at Chapel Hill," he recalled. "Like every two years I returned to Chapel Hill. I was the visiting writer at UNC and at Duke, and I just felt that I was home a lot." In 2004 Kenan was offered a position in the English department at UNC that he couldn't refuse—but the situation was by no means straightforward. At the time, Kenan had moved on from *Walking on Water* and was "sort of gradually [moving] back into fiction. I was publishing short stories in the beginning of what would be a novel." After the events of September 11, 2001, Kenan found himself "homesick for New York, and the plan was for me to go back to Columbia. But then my friend Tom Rankin, who had left Ole Miss to take over the Center for Documentary Study, had made this offer for me to come teach at Duke." At first, Kenan was going to spend only a year in Durham and then head back to New York. But after one semester at the Center, he got a call from his old friend Bland Simpson. He remembered Simpson asking, "If we can pay you what you want will you come over here?" The answer—of course—was yes, and in the winter of 2004 Randall Kenan became an associate professor of creative writing at his old university in the familiar town of Chapel Hill. "It was like Brer Rabbit in the briar patch," Kenan recalled of coming home, even though he admitted to feeling a little apprehensive at first. "A few of my professors were still there. Like Beverly Taylor; she had just started when I was an undergraduate. She was chairman. And Trudier Harris was back."

Kenan continued to flourish. Surrounded by old friends in the early years of his new position, he found Chapel Hill changed for the better: "The thing that I noticed most about the Chapel Hill students is that, when I had been back ten years prior to that in the '90s, there were more students like me. And now they're all from Montclair, Charlotte. They're a sort of more professional student, and I'm spoiled because I get to work with the cream of the crop." Just three years after accepting the job at UNC, Kenan published a collection of essays, *The Fire This Time,* obviously referencing his intellectual mentor James Baldwin, who had published his collection *The Fire Next Time* in 1963. "Dennis Lloyd Johnson, who started Melville House, asked me [to write something] to tie in with the Baldwin Anniversary," Kenan recalled. In 1994, Kenan had written a short biography of Baldwin for Chelsea House, "targeted at gay and lesbian teenagers," and while at Knopf he had also worked with David Leeming on his Baldwin biography. "So I had sort of backed into the Baldwin thing," Kenan concluded.

*The Fire This Time* came out in 2007, and by 2010 Randall Kenan had also finished editing Baldwin's uncollected writings for a book titled *The Cross of Redemption.* That final collection also emerged because of his relationship with Leeming, "who had done the bibliography." Kenan recalled that David Leeming had worked for Baldwin in the '60s. "He was Baldwin's assistant, so he kind of knew where all the bodies were buried. And he had put together—and actually if you look at his biography, at the end of it, he had already done that bibliography—so it, was really a process of just finding all that stuff was based on his work he'd already done."

Since 2010, Kenan has been slowly piecing together a novel: "It's called *There's a Man Going 'Round Picking Names,* and it is about a kidnapping that takes place in 1970, two very privileged young boys, one is black and one is white, and it sort of follows these boys through their growing up." The novel stems from an idea Kenan has carried around with him for a long time, and the composition of it has likewise been piecemeal over the years: "I've published a chapter in *Callilou* and for Vanderbilt." In the late 2010s, Kenan was in the process of drafting—"I mean sort of trying to refine it, to do some rehabilitation, renovation"—and hoping for publication by the end of the decade.

Long a defining voice of the American South, Kenan has become a major international figure in the field of race and region in American culture. His work on James Baldwin and identity only complicates his legacy in fiction. Very few authors can claim to be major figures in both fiction and nonfiction —not to mention scholarly and manuscript work. But Randall Kenan is truly a man of letters, of multiple genres and voices. In the pages that follow, I explore Kenan's best-known contributions to fiction and nonfiction as well as the legacy of his reputation. Perhaps the most difficult part of understanding an author like Randall Kenan is juggling his prodigious skill in so many genres and types of writing. But the first step of the journey must begin with an examination of his first novel, the bold and rapturous *A Visitation of Spirits.*

# CHAPTER 2

## A Community of Ghosts

> "With *A Visitation of Spirits,* it took me a long time to figure out what the novel was really about. I had worked four years on a book that I thought was going to be that novel, and was stumped at one point, and put it down for a long time. There followed a period of months where I didn't physically work on it—unknown to me, I was actually working on it in my mind. I totally restructured the story—consciously and unconsciously—in my brain, and, again, slowly, painstakingly, I tried to start things again. Over the course of months, I came to more clarity."
>
> Kenan in conversation with Charles H. Rowell

Though it's hard to imagine now, almost thirty years ago no one outside a handful of publishing circles in New York City knew who Randall Kenan was. And even those who did knew Kenan only as a hardworking editor with a keen understanding of raw talent. Few knew that Kenan had in him the kind of masterful skill set needed for crafting fiction that would propel him to fame. Ignorance of Kenan's gift lasted until 1992, when his first novel, *A Visitation of Spirits,* was released to major acclaim. First published by Grove Press, Kenan's debut novel garnered critical praise, including some heady back-cover blurbs by the likes of Gloria Naylor and Adrienne Kennedy, the latter of whom commented that Kenan's aesthetic matched "the incandescence and mystery of Alice Walker's short stories."[1]

In his first novel, Kenan introduces his readers to the fictional universe of Tims Creek, a small rural community in North Carolina that Kenan clearly modeled after his own childhood hometown of Chinquapin, North Carolina. There, Kenan examines two central figures—the first, Horace Cross, a sixteen-year-old boy, who, during an already difficult maturation process, recognizes the disconnection between his physical desires and what his community and family desire for him. The second protagonist, Reverend James Greene, Horace's cousin, serves as a kind of foil for Horace. Greene has already completed the complicated process of growing up and consequently has denied the carnal desires that conflict with his religious vocation. When Horace comes to his cousin for advice, he finds only rejection and condescension. Kenan's story shifts between Reverend Greene's plodding daily routine in the winter of 1985 and an investigation of Horace's interior world the spring before, when the boy searched for some way to reconcile his identity with all the expectations imposed upon him.

The framing device for the novel is a five-section structure broken up by chapters titled after the date and time in which they take place (although several of the sections begin with "Confessions" by Greene and Cross). The time switches back and forth from the "present" of December 1985 back to April 1984. Kenan's brief first section, titled "White Sorcery," opens with Jimmy Greene taking his great-aunt and -uncle to visit a sick friend in the hospital. During a conversation about hog butchering, Greene turns inward, and Kenan pens a lyric ode to the magic of the ritual of hog killing in a small, rural town in the south. Interspersed with graphic imagery of the cleansing of the pig ("the creature will be split clear in two, its delicate organs spilling down like vomit" [8]), Kenan presents a more poetic and mysterious explanation for the permanence of memories of old rituals: "the ghosts of those times are stubborn," he concludes (10). After the prosaic exploration of the hog killing, Kenan gives us our first glimpse of Horace, who, frustrated by his mortal identity, has decided to transform himself into an animal. Deciding that his life as a bird would be freest from the burdens of his current human form, he goes to the library to choose the proper species and type from an encyclopedia. The boy eventually decides on a hawk but has second thoughts about his ability to pull off such a mutation. "His was a very rational mind, acquainted with science and mathematics," Horace tells himself. "But he was also a believer in an unseen world full of archangels and prophets and folk rising from the dead" (16). When he travels into the forest to work his sorcery, Horace unwittingly summons and then is possessed by a demon. The section ends with the demon's voice commanding Horace to march forward through the town; the boy obeys, half-naked and carrying his grandfather's gun. Horace begins his journey out into the familiar world of his town "surrounded by hobgoblins and sprites and evil faeries and wargs—aberrations like himself" (28).

In "Black Necromancy," Kenan begins with a written confession from James Greene, the pastor we met in the first chapter of "White Sorcery." In this first chapter of the second section, Greene confesses frankly that he lacks that courage and bravery that he found in his now-dead wife, Anne. Before she passed away from cancer, Greene knew she was the stronger of the two of them and that his curiosity was really "just fear on my part" (36), a fear he senses in his younger cousin, Horace. In the middle of the chapter, Kenan turns from prose to screenplay as he recounts an important meeting between Horace and Jimmy that took place shortly after the action of the second chapter of section one, when Horace was wandering the town possessed by a demon. Greene is still haunted by the memory of seeing Horace in such a state of despair and madness. The second chapter shifts back to the "present" time in December 1985 and a road trip with Aunt Ruth and Uncle Ezekiel (Zeke) to visit their friend, Asa, who is in the hospital.

Kenan spends some time inhabiting each one of his characters' perspectives and working through some of the exposition of the family history of the Crosses. In the final chapter of the second section, Kenan switches back to Horace's dark night of possession as the demon forces Horace to walk down to "his church . . . First Baptist Church of Tims Creek" (68). As he enters, Horace is shocked to realize the church is full of a congregation of spirits from the town but also from the boy's past, including his grandmother and grandfather. "You might call them ghosts. Ghosts of the past," the demon tells Horace. "This is the effluvium of souls that surround men daily. . . . You are seeing. I have removed the scales from your eyes" (73). The congregation of spirits listens to a sermon by the now-deceased Reverend Barden, Jimmy Greene's predecessor. Barden preaches a sermon about being wary of the devil and his minions. After refusing his possessing demon's request that he kill Barden, Horace finds himself baptized by the preacher while the congregation spits invectives at him from below: "Man lover! Child molester! Sissy!" (86–87). He escapes from the church only to stumble upon his old elementary school, where Greene is currently the principal. Looking through a dusty window, Horace watches a scene from his past play out; he has been caught fighting with another child. The chapter ends with Horace's demon compelling him to steal Daisy Sapphire's—Horace's second-grade teacher—car. "We've got places to go before the sun rises," he tells the boy.

"Holy Science" opens with another of Jimmy Greene's "Confessions." In this chapter, we learn that, on June 10, 1983, Horace came to visit his cousin to seek his advice. When the boy confides in Greene that he thinks he's gay, the reverend encourages Horace to not worry about it too much: "Horace, we've all done a little . . . you know . . . experimenting. It's part of growing up . . . it's just a phase. I went through a period where I . . . you know, experimented" (113). However, Greene cannot offer Horace the solace he needs because the boy's sexual identity is not something that is mutable, and he is not going through a phase. "What if I can't change," Horace pleadingly asks his cousin, only to be put off again: "Don't dwell on it too much. You'll be fine" (114). Greene is clearly haunted by this memory of the interaction with Horace, just as he is haunted by his relationship, or lack thereof, with his mother, Rose.

With Zeke and Ruth now visiting Asa in the hospital, Kenan intersperses the scene with memories of fights and hostile conversations between the two characters. Visiting Asa shakes Ruth, who asks herself, "Why is it, Ruth, if you are so firm in your knowledge and knowing, so sure of all these things and not fooled, why is it that you are so unnerved to see your husband's cousin at death's door?" (126). Their praying over Asa keeps being interrupted by the clamoring of the woman who shares the hospital room with him; she doesn't understand where she is or what's happening. Ruth finds herself getting angry at the sick woman's outbursts as they attempt to watch over Asa. Ruth finally finds the words to pray over Asa, but she keeps slipping back into her painful memories of life with Zeke. In the end, Ruth finds she has difficulty forgetting or forgiving her family members for the suffering they have caused her.

Meanwhile, Horace has arrived at the demon's requested destination, South York County High School, and they enter the building and into the boy's memories of the place. Walking among ghosts of his past, Horace recognizes his first love, Gideon, "brown and sweet, as complex as calculus and as direct as a bare fist" (143). The boy remembers their brief affair and how it frightens him into trying to "change" back to a normal, heterosexual boy. And yet, he remembers the constant anxiety over whether he has truly crossed back over: "Had the sinful thoughts left him? Had he become normal? Had he changed?" (161). When Gideon confronts Horace in the locker room after school one day, Horace turns on him. "What we did. What you do is wrong" (162) he tells Gideon. When Gideon tries to seduce him, Horace lashes out and hits him in the face. A wounded Gideon flings back the truth of Horace's sexual identity: "remember, black boy, you heard it here first: You're a faggot, Horace. You know? You're a faggot. You can run, you can hide, but when the shit comes down . . . you suck cock, you don't eat pussy. . . . At least I know what I am" (165). As he retreats from the horrifying visions of his past, Horace sees a dark figure in the middle of the football field and runs towards him; however, he is himself given chase by a group of white men who are shocked to see a naked black man running on campus carrying a gun. Horace gets to his car just in time to escape, but the men follow him. Back in his stolen car, Horace heads out on the road and tries to lose the men following him.

Kenan's penultimate section, "Old Demonology," opens with the final confessions of Jimmy Greene; in the chapter, the preacher admits he has "lied . . .

[to] myself" (172). To explain what those lies mean, Greene goes through the courtship and marriage of his wife, Anne. Even though Anne freely offers her body to her husband, Greene never feels he possesses a knowledge of who she is or what their love means. One day, Greene walks in on Anne having an affair and realizes, with sadness, that his wife does not regret the event, not even in the heat of the moment. Greene's memory shifts to Thanksgiving Day in 1983; everyone at the table is waiting for Horace to come to eat. When the boy arrives with his ear pierced, the family begins to berate him for his appearance and for hanging out too much with white boys. When Horace reacts by calling them all bigots, he is forced to leave the table. Remembering the scene now, Greene realizes that no one knows who they are anymore; it is a sickness that cannot be cured even by faith. "How, Lord? How? How can we defend ourselves and grow strong again?" he wonders out loud (188).

In the next chapter, Jimmy sits with Zeke and Ruth at a diner as they order food and begin to nitpick at each other. When their fight gets out of control, Ruth retreats to the car to cool down. Though Zeke comes to apologize, the two don't reconcile, and, to make matters worse, the car won't start. At a local mechanic's office, Ruth is fascinated by a video game, Pac-Man. When the child playing the game teaches Ruth how to move the little character around the screen, Ruth finds she quite enjoys the game. The peace she gets from playing lasts throughout the car ride home, and Jimmy safely deposits the two back home before turning to drive back to his own house. Meanwhile, Horace listens to the voice of a ghost babble in his ear, even as he escapes the men chasing him. He pulls in to the Crosstown Theater and gets out of his stolen car.

The exhibit at the theater, *Ride the Freedom Star,* is "a lavish production" that ostensibly tells the story of the town's settlers all the way up through the present day. What makes the attraction so compelling, however, is the emphasis on the "picture of domestic bliss" that the author/director creates for "the house slaves and of jolly camaraderie for the field workers" (213). Horace remembers back to a production of *Ride the Freedom Star* that he worked on when he was younger, recalling especially the actors in the show: "the men were mostly gay, which haunted and taunted Horace, for to him they were physically beautiful" (216). But, it is specifically one man, Everett Church Harrington IV, who convinces Horace "that his mind had lied to his heart" (216). Remembering Everett, Horace stumbles backstage into the costume shack and comes face to face with an image of himself in a mirror putting on makeup. This new specter shocks Horace more than any spirit he has seen thus far; the dark double of Horace begins to apply white paint to his face until all his blackness is obscured. When he stands and beckons Horace to sit so that he can apply the same white goo to his face, Horace balks.

Gradually, the image in the mirror shifts from a reflection of Horace to a vision of his affair with another actor in the cast, Antonio, who seduces Horace by telling him he looks a lot like the lover he left behind in New York. Horace watches the important moments of their affair play out in front of him before the mirror shatters. Putting on the garb of an "educated, crusading, reconstructionist minister from the North" (226), Horace exits the costume shack and finds himself caught up in a final reverie. In the vision of the memory he sees, Horace confesses his love for Everett, who rejects him dispassionately. Later, he hears Everett and the director, Edward, caught up in the passion of making love. The memory of that night haunts Horace in ways he cannot begin to explain to himself: "the memory lodged itself in his soul like an unmelting, unmeltable sliver of ice" (231). Lost in the final dream-memory, Horace finds himself at a graveyard hearing the voice of prophecy ringing in his head. The choice he feels laid out for him is simple: to follow the demon in his head or to follow his dark double, who suggests that the only way out is through suicide. Horace fires at the specter but finds he has shot the boy through the chest, the words of Gideon echoing in his ears: "You can run, but you cannot hide" (235). As the voices of his characters subside, Kenan's own appears: "Horace had no alternative but to retreat into a world of guilt and confusion, not understanding the reasons for his exile" (239); the only escape he can possibly imagine for his condition is sorcery.

The final section of *A Visitation of Spirits* opens not with Jimmy Greene's confessions but with Horace's. In the first part of "Old Gods, New Demons," Horace works through his memories of both beautiful and traumatic events, including the first time he saw a chicken killed for dinner, music, comic books, and the pleasure of his physical body. All his memories coalesce around sexual identity: "I remember watching men, even as a little boy. I remember feeling strange and good and nasty. I remember doing it anyway, looking, and feeling that way. I remember not being able to stop and worrying and then stopping worrying. I remember the sight of men's naked waists. I remember the abdomen that looked sculpted and the sinews' definition. Solid. . . . I remember the first picture I saw of a naked man. I remember feeling ashamed. It made me hard" (248).

Remembering those physical desires reminds Horace of his shame, especially in relation to his faith. He ends his confessions by the brutal memory over "worrying that I was not worthy of taking Communion because I was unclean, no matter how much I prayed and asked forgiveness. . . . I remember the day I realized I was probably not going to go home to heaven, cause the rules were too hard for me to keep" (251). Though he bemoans his weakness, it is the strength of Horace's identity that ends his section; he concludes, "I remember me."

In the final chapter of the last section of his novel, Kenan narrates the final moments of Horace's life, as his cousin, Jimmy Greene, tries to reason with the boy to not go through with killing himself. "You're too intelligent . . . to fall for this crap," Greene tells Horace, but the demon, not the boy, responds: "Save it. He knows" (253). Though there is no way of knowing whether Horace is possessed by a demon or an evil spirit, it doesn't matter; he shoots himself in the head. Kenan focuses on the physical details of the suicide rather than what the act means: "these are facts," he tells us. "Whether or not the demon was a ghost of his mind, or a spirit of the nether world, this did happen" (254). In a final, meditative, dreamy section, Kenan shifts away from the narrative he has been writing into a second-person "requiem for tobacco." The section marks a shift in the novel, but its presence mirrors the opening "White Sorcery" section about hog killing, reminding the reader of the cyclical nature of a life built around agriculture and tradition.

### Dark Doubles, Brothers, and Binaries

Perhaps the most striking theme in *A Visitation of Spirits* is Kenan's exploration of doubling. Clearly his two main protagonists are meant to be a kind of double for each other: Horace, the young boy caught between the two poles of his faith and his bodily desires, and Jimmy Greene, who also works through a similar struggle. But the men come to dramatically different conclusions and choose drastically dissimilar paths. Because Kenan's debut novel follows only those two men, we are meant to read their journey as competing narratives in which the decisions and conflicts of both Horace and Jimmy reflect on the trajectory of both. As if to emphasize the importance of their interactions, whenever Kenan presents the two men talking, he ruptures his text, moving from prose to screenplay; their dialogue is at the crux of the novel not just because the plot points are so important but because the interactions help to magnify, reflect, and sometimes distort the other's perspective. Kenan's textual shifting calls attention to his purposeful highlighting of the two men's crucial scenes.

Jimmy reads himself into Horace in several ways; when the boy comes to the minister to confess his love of men, Jimmy responds by replacing Horace's image with his own: "I have reason to believe it's just a phase," he tells Horace. "I went through a period where I . . . you know, experimented" (113). Jimmy Greene is a terrible reader of other people; throughout the novel, he can see others only through how they reflect his identity. And it is his crucial inability to imagine any experience outside of his own perspective that precipitates the tragedies of his life: his wife's affair and Horace's suicide. When Greene walks in on Anne with another man, he cannot process what has occurred because he cannot imagine that his wife is anything but in love with him. Similarly, when Horace confronts him with a gun, Greene cannot help him because he lacks the ability to imagine Horace's capacity for self-violence. Kenan repeats the phrase "I can't believe this" (253) several times before Greene witnesses Horace's cousin kill himself. If Horace is Jimmy's textual dark double, Jimmy Greene's real tragedy is a failure of imagination—he cannot imagine another person unless he is a copy, a mirror image, of himself. As Trudier Harris noted, "Jimmy provides a pathetical example of adult male development" throughout *Visitation*.[2]

Horace, on the other hand, has many spiritual doubles throughout the text. If Jimmy Greene cannot read other people without translating their actions through his own perspective, Horace has almost the opposite problem: he cannot *stop* imagining a multiplicity of voices, eyes, figures, and spirits surrounding him. Toward the end of his dark night of the soul, these spirits coalesce into one form, which comes to Horace as his doppelganger. Sitting down at the table in the costume shack, Horace looks into the mirror; "the face appeared more and more familiar, though it was becoming obscured by milky greasepaint. He realized. Saw clearly. It was him. Horace. Sitting before the mirror, applying makeup" (219). The sudden vision of this doubled version of himself stuns the young man: "Of all the things he had seen this night, all the memories he had confronted, all the ghouls and ghosts and specters, this shook him the most. Stunned, confused, bewildered, he could only stare at his reflection, seeing him and him and him . . . the double stood up. He was exactly the same height as Horace, the same build. . . . They looked at one another, their eyes, the same eyes, trying to peer past the will of the other" (219–221).

Significantly, Horace's double puts makeup all over his face so that it is "finished in a white like porcelain" (220). The mirror image offers the same paint to Horace, but the boy refuses, runs, tries to escape the doppelganger. However, just as Gideon prophesizes, Horace cannot outrun himself or his encroaching anxiety surrounding his friendship with the white students at school. Though he shoots at the double and wounds him, Horace ends up only hurting himself, and the lifeless body of his double on the grass only serves as a further prophecy of Horace's eventual death at the end of the novel. In his last confession, Horace breaks the image of himself into two and remembers significant moments in his life, but his final memory—"I remember me"—reminds the reader that Horace's double life has become literalized. He is no longer one Horace, in body and soul, but now Horace separate in both (dead) body and (living) spirit.

The binary of body/spirit connects with several other binaries that Kenan works through in *Visitation*. Kenan's sections explicitly tie the idea of spirituality with binaries such as black/white ("White Sorcery" versus "Black

Necromancy") and old/young ("Old Demonology" versus "Old Gods, New Demons"). His third section finds a kind of strange connection between what appears to be—at least nominally—another binary: "Holy Science." In the third section, Kenan works through the binary of science/religion as well as his character doubling of Horace/Jimmy. Horace is a man of science; he finds comfort and purpose in facts and figures. Jimmy, however, is a man of faith; he works his "magic" through sermons and by ministering to his congregation. But, just as Kenan connects the dark doubles of Horace and Jimmy, he also unites the world of the seen and the unseen throughout his novel, and the author finds that, in the exploration of the seemingly opposite worlds of science and faith, there is a kind of mystery and magic that can be redemptive.

An anxiety between what can be seen and what must be believed without sight is at the heart of *A Visitation of Spirits*. Horace's possession cannot be "seen," at least not by the outside world. Jimmy refuses to believe that his cousin has been afflicted by demons and spirits. In one of the ultimate ironies of the novel, Jimmy Greene—a man whose profession is based on faith in what cannot be seen—refuses to "believe" that his cousin has been possessed by spirits. His failure to imagine a spiritual world leaves him impotent to speak to/for Horace, and the boy's suicide in front of him leaves the preacher hollow, empty. Kenan connects the seen/unseen binary not only to religion but also to the crucial ideas of memory, both cultural and personal. Because Tims Creek is a community based on tradition, the culture has "memories" that, even though its citizens may not have "seen" with their own eyes, still haunt them as though they had experienced them in the flesh. In his opening section about hog killing, the narrator asks his second person subject several times, "But you've seen this, haven't you?" (9). And its mirror section at the end of the novel—perhaps its own dark double—begins with the same uncertainty about what is "seen" through memory: "You remember, though perhaps you don't" (254). Unseen memories become the basis for a community of "faith," and the unseen certainty of its people creates a haunting series of specters that become literalized in Horace's dark incantations.

### A Community of Ghosts: Spirited Away

The ghosts, ghouls, and spirits that haunt Horace throughout *A Visitation of Spirits* belong to the community of Tims Creek; they are not just visions from one boy's past but specters of an entire community's history. The genre of the novel becomes its own haunting specter—a blended version of magic realism that works to expose the critical failures of Horace's physical community to read, redeem, and, ultimately, save him. Kenan explains:

> The bedrock of what people think of as Southern literature is realism. And as I said, my earliest influences, my earliest fascinations and passions, were for texts that were not bound by what would fit into most people's realism. . . . My great-aunts and uncles would often sit around and talk about ghosts and the spirit world. Demons and the devils were very real things to me, so how could I see the world without them? When I encountered Morrison and when I encountered García Márquez, it was as if they had given me a license to go right on seeing the world the way I saw it. . . . Yet it was a worldview that was not consonant with this political, social realism that I was being instructed to follow. In truth, I don't see social realism and so-called magic realism as being counter. I see them as being able to co-exist. That's what, in my own humble and stumbling way, I attempted to do—interject into the ongoing American dialogue, that social dialogue and that political dialogue, another dimension which was a world of mystery and the unknowable which, for me as a child and to the people around me, was very real and very present, and I wanted to be true to that way of looking at and living in the world.[3]

Kenan's objective correlative for the "haunted history" of the town and its people is the Crosstown Theater's play, *Ride the Freedom Star,* which supposedly documents "A Musical/The saga of an/American Family./Their Trials through the/Revolution,/through the/Civil War/through the trials and hardship/through birth and death/through the tumults and tribulations of love/This is their story/The American Story" (210). The production becomes a local source of pride, even though the "history" it presents of the town is littered with dramatic embellishments and misrepresentations.

In some ways, Kenan seems to connect the idea of *Ride the Freedom Star* and its reworking of familial and cultural history as escapist entertainment with the very function of art itself; reading the advertisement for *Ride the Freedom Star,* one could almost make a case that Kenan boils the trajectory of his novel down to the same kind of endeavor: to tell the story of an American family through "the tumults and tribulations of love." Thinking about *Visitation* as a version of *Ride the Freedom Star* also suggests that the ghosts and specters that haunt Horace throughout the novel are, in some ways, like the characters and events that haunt the reader in the process of working through Kenan's novel. Though we are not present for Horace's interactions with students, lovers, and family the first time around, we "see" the ghost of their interactions reflected through Kenan's prose. In *A Visitation of Spirits,* Kenan suggests that haunting is a trope that connects explicitly with the act of novel writing (and, by extension, novel reading).

The Crosstown Theater also serves as a haunting reminder of Horace's own conflict in the novel, caught between the poles of white/black and family/community. Kenan notes that the theater had been built "with a grant from the Cross Endowment . . . family owned companies." Philip Cross, "the last male of the white Cross line," decides to stage a play at the theater, written by him, "about his illustrious family's history, a stage biography with music" (212). Working on the show, Horace experiences firsthand the way in which his history, the history of his family, and the history of the town all get misrepresented by Phillip; the boy notes "many of the historical facts were just plain wrong" (213). The black characters that Phillip writes "were mainly there for buffoonery and hijinks that brought laughs and chuckles from the audience, for the church scenes, with their raw and dynamic singing, and for the minister's sermon, which was the most passionate, hell-raising moment in the entire play" (213–214). It is not lost on the reader that several of the most important scenes and characters that appear in Kenan's novel also are highlighted by Phillip in his play, especially his "minister" and "church" scenes.

The experience of watching *Ride the Freedom Star* is surreal for Horace both because he is awash with feelings of lust and wonder for the gay actors from faraway cities and also because he must endure a nightly misrepresentation of his identity. When Antonio, one of the actors hired from New York to play a lead, asks him what he thinks of the play, Horace responds:

> Well, it's more than a little inaccurate, to tell the truth. I didn't have a great-great-great-grandfather named Ebenezer.
>
> Damn, you know, I never put two and two together. That's *your* fucking family, too, isn't it?
>
> Sort of.
>
> Shit. Well how does it feel? I bet it makes you mad as hell.
>
> Yeah. Kind of. But . . . I don't know. It's funny. I'm kind of proud, too. You know. Not about the slavery stuff, but to know where we've gotten, you know? (224)

The power of art to distort and misrepresent becomes a way for Kenan to connect his theme of the binary to that of haunting. Here, at the Crosstown Theater, there are literal and symbolic crossings taking place, as opposite poles, ideas, and competing histories come together to create something mysterious. It is at the theater that Horace understands the responsibility given to him by his family and town—"to make my family proud of me" (224)—through the lens of a ghostly performance celebrating black shame. The theater is also where key aspects of Horace's identity—for example, his race and sexuality—resist the binary pull of black/white or gay/straight.

Horace remembers that, on the opening night of the play, he was rejected by the actor he admired the most; stumbling out into a graveyard with the other actors, he finds himself disturbed. That memory haunts the boy: it is "lodged in his soul like an unmelting, unmeltable sliver of ice" (231). In that graveyard, overwhelmed by his feelings of rejection, shame, pride, hopefulness, fear, and boredom, Horace feels a sense of the mystery and magic he desires. The actors assembled there with him are like "witches in a coven under a full moon, like wild wolves tearing hungrily at one another's flesh, like hogs wallowing in their own excrement and sin and lonely inarticulateness" (230). Even though there is the potential for magic, nothing strange or supernatural occurs: "The moon did not change color or phase, lightning did not flash, the earth did not quake, the sun did not rise" (230–231). Whatever promise the haunting memory and the specters of Horace's past offer him leads him to no conclusion other than the morbid embrace of death. Standing in the same spot he had been in with the actors, Horace feels that "suddenly life beneath the ground had a certain appeal it had never had before. It was becoming attractive in a macabre way. No more, no more ghosts, no more sin, no more, no more" (231).

Kenan's playful signifying on Charles Dickens's *A Christmas Carol* is palpable in the scene in the graveyard. Horace has convinced himself that "he knew the outcome of this story, he fully expected to see his own grave" (231), just as Ebenezer Scrooge does at the end of Dickens's famous story when Scrooge is led to a final vision of his death. In fact, much of *A Visitation of Spirits* uses Dickens's narrative to comment on Horace's journey. One of Kenan's epigraphs to the novel comes from the dialogue between Scrooge ("Ebenezer" is the name that Horace will later deny was his great-great-great grandfather's) and the Ghost of Christmas Present, who confides in the old man that he will leave the earth "to-night at midnight." And when Horace is first "visited" by a spirit, the charge he hears is much the same as the one given to Scrooge by the various ghosts he is visited by on Christmas Eve: "the voice said march, so he marched, surrounded by hobgoblins and sprites and evil faeries and wargs—aberrations like himself, fierce and untamed, who frolicked about him with hellish glee at his acceptance of his doomed, delicious fate" (28).

Working through the journey of *A Christmas Carol,* Kenan has his demon-ghost lead Horace first through the boy's past as far back as Horace can remember, into the haunting world of a time before his birth. The first setting of their journey is the First Baptist Church of Tims Creek, where Horace is overcome by memories of his grandparents. He sees his grandmother and tells his spirit guide incredulously:

> She's dead, said Horace. Most of these people are. I . . .
> We all are, boy, said the demon.
> But, how can these people be here? I mean . . . are they ghosts?
> Are you really as dumb as you look? asked the demon. You know, for all your damned learning, you don't know a motherfucking thing, do you? Ghosts? Yeah, you might call them ghosts. Ghosts of the past. The presence of the present. The very stuff of which the future is made. (72–73)

Kenan's demon-ghost uses the very language—past, present, future—of Dickens's spirits that guide Scrooge throughout *A Christmas Carol,* and, just like Scrooge, Horace is given the gift of "seeing" ghosts of his past, visions of his present, and possible specters of his future through a community of ghosts. Like those of Dickens's protagonist, Horace's visions are meant to shock the boy out of his complacency, though Horace's transformation is not the ethical conversion of a miserly old man but rather a potential movement from mortal to ghost. Unable to be the bearer of spirituality for his religious community, Horace must transform into a spirit. Scenes from Horace's past end not with regret and despair, as in Dickens's story, but with the boy's realization that he can no longer belong to a congregation and a community that read him as unclean and wicked. He runs out of the doors of the church while the congregation hurls insults like "Faggot" and "Homo-suck-shual" at him (87). To understand his place in the community, Horace must first embrace his transformation into—what the church would label—a monster.

### (Trans)Forming: "Weird" Mutations and Queer Secrets

The critic Antiwan Walker notes that *Visitation* "clearly encapsulates the thorny intersection of race, history, sexuality, geography, and nationalist politics and the effect it has on Horace's nascent homosexual identity; the novel unveils what happens when what was once taboo and invisible becomes visible and uncovers the effects of silence, erasure, oppression."[4] Visible queerness haunts the novel from its very opening. In the second scene of Horace's *Christmas Carol*-esque journey, he visits himself a little older at elementary (and later high) school. In that space, the boy begins to be haunted by visions of his queerness. It first comes to him through Emma Dobson, who confesses to Horace she finds him "just plain weird" (97). When he presses her on what she means by the word "weird," she falters: "Well . . . I don't know. All you do is read books and stuff. You don't play ball like the other guys. You're just kind of . . . I don't know . . . kind of like Gideon—I mean, you ain't a sissy or nothing—and you're kind of cute, really, but, but . . . shoot, Horace. I just can't be your girl friend! I don't want a boyfriend everybody calls *weird*! Now let me go!" (97).

Horace recognizes the truth of his weirdness: "He wasn't like the other guys." If most of the other boys were out playing football or wrestling one another, Horace was home alone, reading comic books or science textbooks. His strangeness confounds the teachers, his friends, and even his family, who don't recognize in the boy anything they can connect to normal versions of boyhood.

Confronted with his sense of weirdness, Horace decides to use his bizarre sense of "otherness" to transform completely out of his current form. When we first meet the boy in *A Visitation of Spirits,* Horace has already decided to become a new animal; he just wonders, "What to become?" (11). For a boy obsessed with superheroes, Horace decides that the most important aspect of his new identity must be the ability to fly. His first inclination is to become a mutant, like an X-Man. In fact, comic books and superheroes become an important theme for Kenan as he explores his main character's transformation throughout the novel. As Horace ponders how to pull off his transformation, he sits in his room surrounded by posters of "his friends," comic-book heroes watching over him: "On the other walls hung a huge green monster-man so muscled he appeared to be a green lump, with huge bare feet, clad only in tattered purple pants, giving an animal leer; a woman whirling a golden lasso, wearing a brassiere shaped like an eagle and zooming through the air atop an airplane made of glass; a Viking with long yellow hair and bulging muscles, swinging a hammer as large as he, his icy blue eyes flashing a solemn warning" (17).

Superheroes work as a point of fascination for Horace precisely because they are "weird" bodies existing within the confines of a normal world. Mutants like the Hulk and Spider-Man experience the disconnect between feeling like normal men or boys and being extraordinary, with powers that are supernatural and inhuman. Horace situates his fantasy of his transformation within the world of comic books, where "weird" metamorphoses into "special," "powerful." Late in the novel, Horace remembers all his comic-book friends and how he wanted so badly "to be a superhero and first trying to design a suit like Iron Man's so I could fly and then a costume like Batman's so I could look tough" (247). But his fantasy of superhero transformation gets short-circuited by another "weirdness" of his identity, his race. "I remember wanting to be rich and white and respected like Bruce Wayne and invulnerable and handsome like Clark Kent," but those figures don't work for him. Instead, he finds solace in the Black Panther, who is "the first black superhero I had ever seen."

More than anything, Horace expresses a deep terror, an anxiety that won't leave him, that his weirdness is not a power, not a super-mutation that will allow him to fight crime, but an abnormality, a monstrosity that will render him repugnant to the rest of the world. The critic Robert McRuer noted that *Visitation* "goes further than a simple validation or celebration of 'difference.'"[5] Horace cannot celebrate his difference, and Kenan suggests that the boy's internal struggle is rooted in his community's understanding of any deviation from normativity as a threat to the institutions it privileges. Beyond his closeness with his white peers, Horace finds his sexuality abnormal as well. Horace's anxiety over his sexual difference manifests itself to him in the figure of Gideon Stone. When he comes across Gideon, Horace recognizes both the boy's aesthetic charms—he is "without a doubt the prettiest boy in . . . class"—but also an abnormality intrinsic to the boy's identity: "Gideon had, as the old men say, sugar in his blood" (97). Gideon's sexuality isn't a style, a choice. It runs deep; it is, as the community says, in his very blood. Gideon doesn't hide his effeminacy; he celebrates it. Gideon's refusal to be shamed causes Horace both admiration and terror. His weird mutation of playful seriousness baffles Horace, who finds him "as complex as calculus and as direct as a bare fist" (143).

When the two boys are forced together for a science experiment, Horace notes that Gideon himself has mutated again, and the language he uses to describe him is replete with the imagery of maturation: "Over the summer Gideon had changed. His girlish, cute body had been transformed, much like a butterfly emerging from a chrysalis" (146). The transformation is "disturbing" for Horace, who cannot reconcile the "sissified ways" of Gideon with his tall frame, thick arms, and "decidedly manly" waist. Kenan emphasizes Gideon's discordant features to highlight the boy's strangeness; like that of a mutant or a superhero, his "weirdness" provides him with a kind of power that is irresistible to Horace. Kenan highlights his theme of "mutation" and its connection to sexual difference through the subject of Gideon and Horace's science experiment on plant tropism, or the way a plant changes, mutates, because of direct stimuli. After their evening working together, Horace has a sexual dream about Gideon, and he awakes holding both the pleasure of his embrace and the terror of what such a love might mean to his community and family: "That night he dreamed of a particular boy and was filled with a warm and tender feeling. There was also the terror, the familiar question he had refused to acknowledge. It was a horrible voice saying: You must cease this sinful thinking! Are you mad? Do you realize what will happen . . . the real danger . . . only made his obsession seem all the more worthwhile" (153).

Kenan's presentation of the dissonances of Gideon's physicality in relationship to the cognitive dissonance of Horace's desire for his friend yields a decidedly queer outcome. Horace lusts after Gideon, longs to fulfill his desires for touch and pleasure, and yet Horace also experiences a destructive shame over their blossoming romance. It is the cognitive dissonance between a physical pleasure and an interior shame because of Horace's community's reading of pleasure that makes Kenan's novel what Walker calls "a conscious critique of hetero-Christianity on the black queer subject."[6]

Once consummated, Horace finds another, subtler change occurring inside himself. He cannot bear to be around Gideon anymore, and his final mutation frightens Horace more than his initial weirdness: "What had changed him? Could he have swung so far in such a short time. . . . Suddenly he became fully aware of his responsibilities as a man, and the possibilities of his being a homosexual frightened him beyond reason" (156). Gradually, Horace begins to convince himself that this new change is a welcome move toward living a normal teenage life. He thinks to himself, "Had the sinful thoughts left him? Had he become normal? Had he changed? There was nothing to change . . . his mind said. You're normal" (161). When Gideon confronts Horace about his aloofness, the "change" he feels connects to his maturation as Gideon notes the developing muscles in his back—"My, oh my, but you're doing some developing" (162). Kenan's exploration of queer mutation, including his working through of plant tropism, comic books, superheroes, and the power of strangeness, all connect to Horace's entrance into puberty, a time when his body is literally transforming. His body is in the midst of a literal physical transformation; even as his mind remains locked between two poles, boyhood and adolescence, spirituality and physicality, playfulness and literalness, Horace's body is that of both a boy and a man. Caught between two competing physical and psychological poles, Horace is never allowed to embrace any marker of his identity and claim his power. He cannot choose his queerness because to do so would invalidate his familial, religious, and community identity. And yet, he cannot claim his religious identity without invalidating his physical desires. Even though he tries violently to reject his queerness, telling Gideon "What you do. It's wrong" (162) and hitting the boy in the face, Horace's desire for men and boys does not disappear.

The "weirdness" of these queer mutations that Kenan emphasizes throughout *A Visitation of Spirits* directly relates to what is unspoken. Horace is terrified that the other boys will know his deepest desires, and he guards his secret sexuality the way Clark Kent guards his identity as Superman. But the tragedy of Horace Cross is that, even in secret, the boy finds he cannot hide his desires from himself; he cannot keep his secret from the voices in his head. When, at the end of his long, haunted night, Horace finally finds an object to enact his redemption, it is not surprising that it is a mysterious "thing" that exists in contradictory form; the language Kenan uses to describe it is the language of dissonance itself: "He saw what he had led himself to see, the reason, the logic, the point. It was round and square. It was hard and soft, black and white, cold and hot, smooth and rough, young and old. It had depth and was shallow, was bright and dull, took light and gave light, was generous and greedy. Holy and profane. Ignorant and wise. Horace saw it and it saw Horace, like the moon, like the sea, like the mountain—so large he could not miss it, so small he could barely see it. The most simple, the most complex, the most wrong, the most right" (232).

Even as Horace understands "where he fit" (234) between the poles suggested by this object, he ultimately rejects his place. He cannot occupy a space in the middle, and, overcome by his "weirdness," his twoness, his duality in the face of a binary world, he "had no alternative but to retreat into a world of guilt and confusion" (239). Significantly, the final act of his "treason" (238) against his family comes not from his embracing of his sexual identity but in their reading of his embracing of whiteness.

When Horace begins to hang out with the white kids at school, he suffers insults that suggest a different kind of mutation, that of color: "Oreo, Greyboy" (238). But his family's rejection of his new friends stings the most. Horace has bought into the "singular, infectious freedom . . . [and] entitlement" (237) of his white friends, but the boy's family commands him to stop hanging out "with them no-account white boys" (239). As Harry Thomas noted, "in addition to being inappropriate in terms of both sexuality and gender, Horace further upsets his caretakers by violating their communal rules concerning race relations. Thus, he is triply queer."[7] The final rejection of Horace's identification with a strangeness, a mutation, is too much for the boy to bear. "What does a young man replace the world with, when the world is denied him?" Kenan seems to ask directly of his reader. And even though Horace makes one last, desperate escape from the binary-loving world of Tims Creek through his superheroes, the stories all ring hollow: "He turned to his comic books; perhaps there he could discern the way out—among the friends he had made years ago when he first learned to read" (240). But that escape offers him connection only with the human alter egos of powerful heroes, not Superman but "Clark Kent, slipping into phone booths," not Batman but "Bruce Wayne" (240). Unlike those heroes, Horace cannot assume the mantle of his power simply by changing clothes. Drowning in a sense of his strangeness and unable to transform himself into a being that either he or his community can recognize as intrinsically valuable, Horace does the only thing he can think of to rectify his situation: to transform from a physical being to a spirit through suicide.

Horace's decision to kill himself is the crux of *A Visitation of Spirits,* and even as Kenan emphasizes the importance of mutation and transformation in Horace's mind, he signifies the importance of transformation in his very prose. The key moments of Horace and Jimmy's interactions are highlighted by a shift from prose to screenplay. The first break from Kenan's prose comes in "Black Necromancy," when Jimmy remembers encountering Horace early in the morning on April 30, 1984, when the boy kills himself. Kenan's scene is an intense standoff between a gun-toting Horace and his fact-wielding cousin, and its intrusion during Jimmy Greene's confessional feels oddly out of place. There is no introduction to the break in the text, and when the scene ends, there is no explanation as to why it is in a different form. It is as if a memory breaks into Jimmy's mind as he listens to the sound of children playing, and then the memory disappears quickly. Kenan suggests that the act of remembering works on his characters like a kind of mutation of time and history, as if everything that ever happened never goes away but works itself into the very fabric of an eternal present. While Greene listens to the sound of children outside his window, inside he is listening to the story of a possessed Horace, himself a mutation of the cousin he knows and the demon who speaks for him. "My name ain't Legion," the possessed Horace tells Jimmy. "Cause I ain't many. But I suspect you get the picture, Preacher-boy" (43).

The second break into screenwriting comes during a time when Greene suddenly remembers Horace coming to him to confess his love for men. As in the first break, the screenplay appears out of the blue and then ends suddenly. Just as in the first screenplay scene, the subject is Horace's anxiety over his transformation. He confides in his cousin that he feels he is changing into something evil. When Greene assures Horace that it is just a phase, that the boy will come to his senses, Horace begs his cousin to answer the question "What if I can't change?" (114). He asks the question twice, but Greene doesn't have a satisfying answer; he only counsels Horace to not "dwell on it too much." The third screenplay scene takes place during another of Greene's memories, this time about the infidelity of his wife, Anne. As he remembers catching her with another man and the emotional conclusion of that time (ending with him vomiting), Greene's consciousness suddenly shifts to Thanksgiving dinner in 1983. The importance of the scene around the dinner table isn't immediately apparent until we reach Horace's chapter at the end of the section "Old Demonology."

In the Thanksgiving scene, the anxiety over changing comes not from within but from outside. Horace arrives to dinner with his ear pierced, and his family reads the new jewelry as a direct affront to everything they value. Accusing Horace of hanging out too much with his new white friends, they also attack his lack of respect for his race and masculinity. Jonnie Mae says, "No better sense than to go on and follow whatever them white fools do. You'd follow them to hell, wouldn't you. . . . He *just* pierced his ear. Like some little girl. Like one of them perverts" (184). When Horace calls them all bigots, he is banished from the table and forced upstairs to his room. Though Greene promises to talk to Horace, he cannot think of anything monumental to say. The significance of the moment hits Greene as the memory ends, and Kenan transforms his writing from screenplay to prose again, as the preacher concludes, "This is what finally got to Horace, isn't it?" One critic noted that Horace, "even as he is aware of the community more as a being than a word . . . also knows that his expulsion from it is a kind of death."[8] Greene's ultimate conclusion about Horace's tragedy connects to the boy's inability to exist as himself and as the community wants him to be: "He, just like me, had been created by this society. He was a son of the community, more than most. His reason for existing, it would seem, was for the salvation of his people. But he was flawed as far as the community was concerned. First, he loved men; a simple, normal deviation, but a deviation this community would never accept. And second, he didn't quite know who he was. That, I don't fully understand, for they had told him, taught him from the cradle on. I guess they didn't reckon the world they were sending him into was different from the world they had conquered, a world peopled with new and hateful monsters" (188).

It is significant that Greene's conclusion ends with "monsters" because Horace's transformation into adolescence has turned him, Frankenstein-like, not into a superhero but into a monster that must be chased out of respectable society. In analyzing the Thanksgiving scene, Trudier Harris concluded, "Horace's family renders him 'Other' by finally making him feel worse than a stranger. They would embrace and feed a stranger. They cannot, will not, embrace the homosexual Horace."[9] Forced to deny his sexuality, and then his desire for community outside his race, Horace can find no world in which he belongs. Unable to live in the real world of his town and family and unable to escape into the fantasy world of his comic-book heroes, Horace concludes that the only place left for him is the world of spirits and ghosts. "It's like the boy wants off the roller coaster ride," the demon tells Greene. "He don't like life, see. Too many fucking rules. Too many unanswered questions. Too many loose ends. You see, life the way Horace wants it ain't condoned, you know what I mean? And condonation—if that's what you call it—is what he wants" (252–253).

### Un-Imagining the Community

Kenan juxtaposes Horace's restless quest for "condonation" and peace with the world of Jimmy Greene and his family. While Horace goes on a spiritual journey to examine his life and transform into something valuable, Greene does very little soul searching. In fact, his physical journey in the novel literally goes nowhere. As Horace encounters sprites, faeries, ghosts, ghouls, and witches,

Greene transports Ezekiel and Ruth to visit Asa in the hospital; on the way back to Tims Creek, his car breaks down. The three of them are trapped for a while in a mechanic's office before they are finally delivered back home. The two men's journeys could not be more different: Horace goes on an epic adventure that tests the limits of his soul, and he comes through it transformed. Jimmy Greene goes in a circle between his home and a nearby town, and he returns blithely unchanged.

If Horace's tragedy is that he exists as two irreconcilable versions of himself—one true to his desires and dreams, true to his family and community—Greene's tragedy is that, long ago, he decided to kill off the part of himself that desired anything other than what the community asked of him. He is completely detached from his emotions. For a man of faith, Jimmy Greene is profoundly unimaginative, locked in a cell of disbelief, anxiety, and fear. Though his professor at seminary tells him that he has the gift of "curiosity," Kenan presents Greene throughout *A Visitation of Spirits* as a man profoundly devoid of true imagination. "No, I thought, I have no idea what you mean," Greene imagines him telling the seminary professor, "for this was no straightforward, textbook theology. I could not simply apply Hegelian logic. And I was not prepared for a mystical, mumbo-jumbo assault so like the superstitious Call for which I had been groomed" (34). Jimmy Greene becomes a preacher not because he is called but in response to "just fear on my part" (36), and he finds himself drastically misdiagnosed by his seminary professor: "Horace . . . had something more, that damned curiosity . . . with a capital C."

Kenan offers Greene possibilities for imagination; for example, it's clear that Jimmy Greene is haunted by the morning when Horace killed himself in front of him. The preacher keeps "thinking there was something I could have done. Said. If not that morning then before, long before . . . but that's just me being a romantic" (36). Even in retrospect, Greene cannot imagine a way that he could have helped Horace, and he is haunted by "images, dark and murky, symbols of indecision and doubt." Staring at the woods where Horace killed himself, Greene can imagine only "futility and waste. As if the very air had become fetid and rank" (40). Even though Kenan offers Greene the opportunity to imagine new ways of changing the past to transform his future, the man falls into empty routine and impotent rituals: "Then it's back to bed," he says of his normal days, "which in many ways seems the object of leaving bed in the first place" (44).

The futility of cycles becomes an important trope for Jimmy Greene throughout his central journey in the novel. When we get a glimpse into the mind of Zeke, we find that it, too, is a jumble of memories and introspection, a cycle of repeating images that only affirm the old man's belief structure. We learn that Zeke's infidelities are just as scandalous as Horace's imagined transgression, but the old man refuses to feel sorry for them: "he got needs, well, maybe they ain't needs, but they are mighty powerful wants. And I declare if you wants something enough in your mind it becomes a need. I ain't ashamed" (60). While Greene and Zeke's lack of imagination allows them to refuse regret as an option, it also crucially forecloses the ability for true communication and growth. Both Zeke and Greene are incapable of change, trapped in the cell of themselves and forced to interact with just the ghosts of their memories, which serve only to entrench their perspective. When Zeke turns his thoughts to Horace, all he can remember is his inability to understand the boy: "he was foreign to me" (64). Zeke has no imagination beyond the borders his culture and family have created for him.

A lack of imagination leading to the inability to communicate is the hallmark of interactions among Greene, Zeke, and Ruth. When the three characters talk, they don't actually *say* anything, and they make no effort to reach out to one another or to see things from a different perspective. "How could I communicate," Greene asks himself as he's visiting some parishioners, "that I was not, did not want to be the holy and pious dictator of a pastor that they had been used to for all of their lives" (110). Instead of envisioning ways to speak from his heart and confess what he truly believes, Greene retreats to his taciturn stillness. When he is given the one true opportunity of his life to actually "minister" to someone he can truly help—Horace, who comes to him with a confession and a desperate need for advice—the preacher fails to communicate anything to his cousin. And, in the other crucial moments in his life, when given the opportunity to reach out to his cheating wife and to the mother who abandoned him, Jimmy Greene is a silent block of stone. As he stands next to Rose at the funeral for his grandmother, he "could feel my heart ossifying within my living breast. It would break before it would soften" (122).

The entire Cross family seems to have a similar lack of imagination that leads to the hardening of their hearts; if Horace's journey mirrors that of Ebenezer Scrooge in *A Christmas Carol*, Kenan suggests that Scrooge's real heirs are Zeke, Ruth, and Greene: they lack the kindness of heart and generosity of spirit that Scrooge also lacked, leading to the visits by the ghosts on Christmas Eve. Perhaps the only redeeming figure in the family is Ruth, who, confronted with the dim vision of a dying Asa, moves from her selfish reveries about her pain to ask the Lord to "take his suffering from him and put it on me" (134). And yet Ruth is a victim of her own lack of imagination, too; she is fiercely territorial about her family, and she never forgets when she has been slighted. Ruth's need for revenge and her memory of suffering turn her into a nasty and mean-spirited woman. When Greene, Zeke, and Ruth go to a diner after visiting the hospital, the family dynamic devolves into chaotic accusations and name calling. Even as Greene tries to "minister" to his own family, he is impotent to help them; he falls back on his lack of imagination and berates them: "Listen to you both. A deacon and a mother of the church . . . I don't believe it. I just don't believe it. That two people who've lived as long and who have been through as much as you two can act so petulant and childish. It's ridiculous" (200). Kenan clearly asks the reader to recall the other time we heard Greene protest his lack of belief: the scene when Horace is about to kill himself.

The tragedy of Horace Cross is that he is forced to exist within a community that defines itself by its lack of imagination; it is a tragedy of setting, not of character. In conversation with V. Hunt, Kenan suggested that the structure of the novel is, at its base, built around a tragic inability to recognize Horace's difference as valuable: "I really liked Aristotle's *Poetics*. I like the things he has to say about tragedy, and what tragedy can do. In terms of [Horace's] situation, if you're looking at it [coming out] from a political angle—which is what I do at the very last moment—the situation has not gotten that much better. For a lot of people. It seemed, and it seems—because I think it is still true that for that community to change they have to understand the devastation that they're wreaking on certain people. And I felt that tragedy was much more effective at disturbing, and moving, people."[10]

Kenan suggests that Horace's family members are incapable of true communication because they cannot understand anything outside their perspective and are haunted and corrupted by their memories of being wronged and by the narratives they've built of their victimization. Greene feels abandoned by his mother, Rose; Ruth hangs onto the pain of never having been accepted by the Cross family; and Zeke cannot forgive those who trespass outside his realm of cultural and ethical understanding. "Do you understand what forgiveness is?" Zeke asks Greene, before confessing, "It takes a right smart man to forgive, and I'll tell you, boy. I don't know if this old man is enough. Strong enough, to walk the way I ought" (206). At a critical moment in Zeke's life, when he needs ministering to more than ever, Greene cannot think of anything to say. "You're supposed to be *my* preacher," he reminds him, but they end up talking about the weather instead.

In the end, Kenan's *A Visitation of Spirits* becomes a powerful condemnation of the power of the unimaginative to wreak a crippling violence on those who are sensitive enough to imagine a world beyond the limits of their family and community. The novel becomes, for one critic, "a means by which we can continue (queerly) pushing toward the center, away from margins that are dark, unfair, that are, I would dare say, unconstitutional, and thus, un-American."[11]

Horace's trespasses are more transgressions of thought than action, and his brutal banishment and rejection by his family lead him to consider another world where he can exist as he imagines himself. The great tragedy of the novel is that Horace's saving grace, the brightly imagined world he longs for, turns out to be the land of the dead.

# CHAPTER 3

## Speaking for/Speaking to the Dead

> "I was planning to include 'Let the Dead Bury Their Dead' in *A Visitation of Spirits*. My first novel could be called a triptych. It was originally conceived as a diptych. It was, at one time, going to have four sections. But at some point I said, people are going to look at this and say: This Negro has lost his natural mind."
>
> Kenan in conversation with V. Hunt

Kenan's second—and thus far most recent—book-length work of fiction came out in 1992 to near universal acclaim. If *A Visitation of Spirits* announced Randall Kenan as a fiction writer whose career was about to take off, *Let the Dead Bury Their Dead* made good on that promise. Nominated for both the National Book Critics Circle Award in Fiction and the *Los Angeles Times Book Award* for fiction, *Let the Dead Bury Their Dead* was also named a *New York Times* Notable Book of the Year and the winner of the Lambda Award. Suddenly, writers and critics for whom Kenan had worked as an editor saw the true potential of the author they had worked with in a variety of different capacities. Terry McMillan called Kenan "a genius; our black [Gabriel García] Márquez. He weaves myth, folktales, magic, and reality like no one else I know, and doesn't miss a beat."[1] In his review, "The Ghosts on Main Street," for the *New York Times,* Howard Frank Mosher wrote, "Randall Kenan's second work of fiction is nothing short of a wonder-book: one of those striking literary anomalies, in the tradition of 'Raintree County' and 'The Country of the Pointed Firs,' that are nearly as difficult to classify as they are enjoyable to read and reread."[2]

Though not a novel, *LTDBTD* works through a trajectory of characters, themes, motifs, and secrets that are all tethered to a single place, Tims Creek, the setting of Horace Cross's dark night of the soul in *Visitation* and Kenan's postage stamp of earth. The true success of Kenan's weaving together disparate stories comes in his exploration of space and the consequences of home. Mosher concludes, "In the end, however, it is the flesh-and-blood residents of Tims Creek who remain with us after we've laughed over their last outrageous exploits and shaken our heads in pure wonderment over their resilience in the face of about the worst life has to offer. Mr. Kenan's dead cannot be discounted. . . . Fiercely and relentlessly, hilariously and sympathetically, Randall Kenan unfolds layer upon layer of the interlocked existences of his Tims Creek citizens. In 'Let the Dead Bury Their Dead' he has created, in a single obscure hamlet, a deeply and peculiarly American community, as memorable as any I have encountered in recent fiction."[3]

It might not be an exaggeration to claim that *LTDBTD*'s success worked to turn more readers onto Kenan's first novel and entrenched *Visitation*'s success. Randall Kenan's achievement with the 1992 collection made him a prominent writer who demanded the attention of the American readership, and his resolve to sell *LTDBTD* as a two-book deal with *Walking on Water* ultimately proved fruitful. In *A Visitation of Spirits,* Kenan had found his home; in *Let the Dead Bury Their Dead,* he found his voice.

### "Clarence and the Dead (And What Do They Tell You Clarence? And the Dead Speak to Clarence)"

Kenan's opening story in the collection begins on the day its titular character, five-year-old Clarence Pickett, dies. Coincidentally, Wilma Jones's frog also stops talking to her on the same day; Clarence's death is part of a day of mystery that connects to the boy's birth as his mother died in labor: "they say that day the sun shone while the rain poured," the narrator explains (1). Like Faulkner's "A Rose for Emily," Kenan's story is told from a third-person point of view by an unidentified "we," who functions, in many ways, as the voice of the town itself. Clarence is marked as special; there is no caul over his head, though "the caul seemed to be everywhere" (2). No one much thought anything about the small boy; it wasn't until he was three years old and began to talk that the town began to take notice of his difference. Instead of piecing together broken English, Clarence, who in his toddlerhood had not "yet said a blessed word" (4), began to speak in complete sentences.

A local farmer, Ed Phelps, finds Clarence in his field one day talking to buzzards, and, after having to kill one of the birds to scare the others away, Ed delivers the garrulous boy back to his astonished family. The town is further shocked that Clarence seems to be able to communicate with the dead, telling Emma Chaney that her deceased mother has a message for her about Chaney's cheating lover, Joe Hattan. But Clarence's talent isn't just for speaking to the dead: he can do all sorts of things, like "announcing 'Such and such a person's going to die today,' or 'Such and such a person died last night'" (6). Clarence tells one person where they left an old insurance policy they'd lost, "another where they mislaid their keys" (6). What terrifies the town, though is that "Clarence told people things a four-year-old boy ain't had no business knowing the language for, let alone the circumstances around them" (8).

The boy's "queer knowledge" culminates in his relationship with Ellsworth Batts, a "good and hard worker who did an odd job now and again for beer money" (150). The boy tells Ellsworth that his now-dead wife wants him "to return to the living folk. She says you have an eternity to be dead. You love too much. . . . There's more to life than love" (16); hearing this, Batts becomes obsessed. The boy sets "off something deep in Ellsworth," who follows Clarence all over town (18). At Clarence's house, Ellsworth begs to speak to the boy, and Clarence's family notes that he looks at their son in the way "a grown man [shouldn't look at] . . . a five-year-old-boy" (18). Batts keeps coming back to the house; he sobers up and arrives in fancier clothes. When he starts to bring Clarence flowers, the notion of a grown man courting a little boy becomes too scandalous to tolerate. George Edward talks to Ellsworth and asks him to stop coming around to the house for fear of "fermenting depraved intentions for young and tender boys" (19). Ellsworth gets bolder in his treatment of Clarence: he kisses the boy, and even, one night, sneaks into his bed to sleep with him. He kidnaps Clarence a week later and, during a chase, jumps off a bridge into a dry river, where he dies of a broken neck. Not long after, the boy dies of a mysterious sickness. The town believes Clarence's death to be an omen: "We figured there was more to it than that, something our imaginations were too timid to draw up, something to do with living and dying that we, so wound up in harvesting corn, cleaning house, minding chickenpox, building houses, getting our hair done . . . really didn't care about or have time or space to know. Why mess in such matters?—matters we really didn't believe in in the first place, and of which the memory grows dimmer and dimmer every time the sun sets" (22).

At Clarence's funeral, a herd of deer stands sentry as the boy is buried.

### "Things of This World; (or, Angels Unawares)"

Kenan's second story starts in Mr. John Edgar Stokes's front yard, where a man lies motionless, face down, next to a crepe myrtle. When Stokes goes to inspect the man, he realizes he is "A Chinaman. Just like he had seen on TV. Look at them eyes, he thought. Just as slanted as a cat" (26). Stokes brings the wounded man into his kitchen and starts to cook soup for his injured guest, who begins to come around. The stranger introduces himself as "Chi" and tells Stokes he is passing through Tims Creek "to see a friend" (29). Chi refuses any medical help and tells Stokes that he had simply fallen; no one had attacked him. Stokes decides to believe the stranger, though he is curious when Chi calls him by his name even though Stokes had never told him who he was. Chi continues to act strangely around Stokes, never telling Mr. John Edgar anything about himself and rising early in the morning to perform a strange, ritualized dance in the front garden. Still, Stokes enjoys the company and doesn't ask Chi any questions. He wants to be polite to his new guest.

One morning after Chi has been with Stokes for a few days, Joe Allen comes around with the body of Stokes's dog, Shep. The "Terrell boys" have apparently killed the dog for "shitting in their yard and . . . chasing a heifer" (35). Stokes solemnly buries the dog, goes into his house, and reemerges with a shotgun. Before Joe Allen can stop him, Stokes is off to exact revenge. With Chi, Joe Allen hops in his truck, and the two go after Stokes, following him to the Terrell General Store. Stokes pushes aside the white Terrell boys on the front porch and, shoving aside Percy Terrell, takes aim and shoots one of "Percy's prize coon dogs," who are yapping at the commotion. Stokes escapes unharmed; Joe and Chi follow him home, and when the sheriff comes to arrest him, Mr. John Edgar points the gun at him and tells him to leave his land. Stuck, the sheriff says, "The law says you got to come with me." "Well," Stokes replies, "the Bible say, 'an eye for an eye,' don't it . . . that's the onliest Law I'm studying about" (42–43). The sheriff calls in backup, and eventually the police take Stokes into custody.

The next day Stokes gets out on a $500 bond, and he is met by his new friend, Chi. Back home, Stokes and Chi sit together talking about how quickly one's life can change. Stokes finds himself "troubled yet transformed . . . amazed to now be awaiting a hearing, a trial. It had come up all of a sudden like a summer storm" (47). Sitting with Chi, Stokes confesses that he hated to kill Terrell's dog; he didn't want to do it. But, he also confesses, "it sho was worth it. Worth it to see the look on that ole Terrell's face. I stood up to that cocksucker" (48). In his final act of confession, Stokes admits he wishes he could "Die. Die right now to spite his sorry ass. Yes sir. To show he ain't got no power over death. Yes sir. I could die right now—content. . . . Sho nuff could. With pleasure" (48).

When Chi asks whether the man could truly die happy right at this moment, Stokes confirms that he is at peace. The next day, they find Stokes dead, "his eyes stretched wide with astonishment, his mouth a gaping O . . . as if his last sight had been something more than truly remarkable, something wonderful and awful to behold" (48). Chi has vanished.

**"The Foundations of the Earth"**

The story opens on the front porch of Maggie MacGowan Williams's house, where the woman sits with Reverend Hezekiah Barden; Henrietta Fuchee, the music teacher at First Baptist; Emma Lewis, Maggie's housekeeper; and a "special guest" (50), Gabriel. We learn that Gabriel is Maggie's grandson Edward's lover; Edward disappeared from his family's life soon after he went away to Boston University. A truck hit his car one rainy night in Springfield, Massachusetts, and Edward was killed, at the age of twenty-seven. Gabriel comes to Maggie almost as "an interpreter for the dead" (56) to tell her about her grandson. Maggie recalls that at first she burned with an intense anger against Gabriel and all he represented, but during a significant dream right after Edward's funeral she began to soften. In her dream, Maggie imagined herself as Job questioning God and being reprimanded for her lack of imagination: "Where wast thou when I laid the foundations of the earth?" God shoots back at the old woman when she asks why he had to take Edward away.

As Gabriel amusedly watches the drama of the town from Maggie's front porch, the reverend decides to go to Morton Henry and scold him for plowing the field on a Sunday. Maggie enlists Gabriel to go referee the spectacle, and as they walk together, she realizes God is calling her to expand her imagination beyond her provincial perspective: "At that moment she understood that she was being called on to realign her thinking about men and women, and men and men, and even women and women" (63). She questions Gabriel about his identity, and the old woman legitimately tries to understand what it means to be gay. Gabriel tells Maggie that he is a normal person with a hard lifestyle that he has been born into, that Edward kept his sexuality from her for fear of being rejected, and all the while Maggie longs only for the young man to "go ahead and tell her what to think: *We're perverts* or *You're wrong-headed, your church has poisoned your mind against your own grandson*" (65).

Maggie's understanding of Edward and Gabriel's love connects to her own deep need for Edward in her life. She finds a connection with Gabriel in the strangest of ways: in Gabriel's need for her grandson, she recognizes her own deep longing for something "to moor her to the Earth" (69). With that connection in mind, she finally begins to forgive Edward and love Gabriel, for "in a world not real, is there truly guilt in willing reality to cohere through the life of another? Is that such a great sin?" she asks herself. When the party finally arrives at Morton's tractor, Maggie is asked to tell the young man to stop his sinful Sabbath plowing. However, she simply tells Morton that he should do whatever he needs to do. Standing up for the man against the wishes of the reverend is liberating, and as they all walk back together Maggie muses on the curious way her world has turned, "that she would be asking a white man to exonerate her in the eyes of her own grandson" (72).

**"The Origin of Whales"**

Kenan's next story also opens on a porch scene, this time the porch of Aunt Essie as she's waiting for her young relative, Thad, to arrive. The boy's mother is attending a convention, and Essie has agreed to watch her son while she is away. Stern and dour, Aunt Essie makes the boy toe the line, but she also plays with him. They take turns being "it" in Hide-N-Seek, and Essie makes the boy a mess of collard greens and cornbread. As the boy eats, Essie regales him with a story about the time her brother, Hugh, ate an entire pot of collard greens. Trying to hide his naughtiness, Hugh told his father that he had seen a bear eat them, and when the skeptical dad took his boy out to find the tracks, both were shocked to find fresh prints. Later that night, Hugh had severe gastrointestinal distress caused by his decision to eat the entire pot of collards, and when he finally went to the outhouse to relieve himself, he woke the house with his screams: he believed that he had seen a bear. Essie assures Thad that there was never a bear, just a frightened little boy.

After supper, Essie helps Thad with his homework; the boy is studying evolution. He explains to Essie, "This says that all animals began as lower animals and adapted into what they are now. . . . Whales even were supposed to walk on the earth with legs and stuff once upon a time" (85). Thad asks Essie if she believes such things; she emphatically maintains that she most certainly does not. When a telephone call interrupts their homework time, Essie retreats to the porch to rock silently. Thad follows eventually and sits next to her. He puts a hand out, wanting to hold Essie's "pecan-colored, large-veined" hand, but draws it back to his chest in a fist.

**"Cornsilk"**

Kenan's first-person story begins with "the smell of blood" (88) and Aaron's—the narrator's—longing for a specific woman's body and blood. Now, feeling useless at his law firm, Aaron finds his joy only at night, when he changes into something different, a monster of sorts, lusting after memories of bodies and the carnal pleasures he must deny himself during the day. During his tumult of confessions, Aaron remembers that his father once told him that corn must be planted with three seeds in one hole so that when the plants grow up there will be "another plant close enough to fertilize the next. Their pollen is heavy. . . . They need to be close. . . . Must be nice" (91). Somehow the idea of corn in rows fills Aaron with another kind of longing, a desire for closeness and intimacy and meaning that constantly elude him.

The reader slowly understands that the specific body Aaron longs for is that of his sister Jamonica, with "her mulatto hue" (91). "I know it sounds Freudian; but it is not Freudian, not Freudian in its intent, though perhaps in its execution" (92), Aaron muses about his condition. Sounding more and more like the narrator of a Poe short story, Aaron wonders aloud whether he is crazy and then spends a large section of his story detailing his history with Jamonica, including one moment that haunts him to this day. He remembers boys visiting Tims Creek from the Bronx and how they surrounded him and Jamonica as they were walking home. The narrator tried to protect his sister but failed and had to watch in horror as the three boys took Jamonica into the corn fields. Thinking he could become a comic book hero, the kind he loved so much, Aaron went into the cornfields "ready to slip into my costume . . . and deliver my sister from harm" (101); instead, he found one of the boys in the midst of making love to his sister. He tried to stop it but was slapped down by Jamonica. Chastened, he returned to Miss Jesse to tell on his sister, but Aaron was reprimanded for being a tattletale. No one ever mentioned the event again, though Aaron secretly holds the memory close, pretending he is the one making love to his sister in the cornfield.

Aaron and Jamonica finally consummate their love one night when the boy is nineteen and his sister is twenty-five. After that, the two cannot stop engaging in wild, passionate sexual escapades: "We practically lived in bed after that. . . . Precious, sinful freedom. Wild positions. I learned much that week. I long to be able to forget it all and return to ignorance" (107). Soon after the consummation of their love, Jamonica tells Aaron they must call off the whole thing. Recognizing there is no happy end game to an incestuous relationship, Jamonica tells her brother that what they are doing is wrong and needs to stop. Tortured by his sudden loss of the source of his sexual awakening, Aaron changes his major to prelaw, disappears into a boring profession, and spends his nights trying to find something—anything, including prostitutes and call girls—that can remind him of what he and his sister shared. He is ultimately unsatisfied, and sticks to his memories and fantasies. In one of Aaron's most potent fantasies, his father and mother walk in on Aaron and Jamonica in the middle of their lovemaking, and they "approve. They throw a party. They tell everyone. . . . I tell my dad I love him. . . . Talk about wish fulfillment" (114).

### "The Strange and Tragic Ballad of Mabel Pearsall"

The titular hero of Kenan's tale is a long-suffering schoolteacher. When we first meet her, she narrowly avoids plowing her car into a deer running across the road. She thanks Jesus for allowing her to escape the near-accident unharmed, but her mind drifts back to a time earlier in the day when she was called into the principal's office. The ugly white principal, Mr. Todd, blows smoke at Mabel and asks if she's feeling okay—he's been receiving complaints that she has been acting strangely. At home, Mabel is treated with little respect by her children and husband, and she begins to feel a sense of sadness and sorrow creeping into her life. "She feels exactly like a child on a ride. A high scary ride. She wants to get off so desperately. Whom does she tell? She starts to pray. Then stops. No one is listening" (126). Mabel finds some relief in her television programs; she knows "it is only fantasy. But such fun. The good are clearly good. The bad badly bad . . . always nice to look at" (128).

Waking up the next morning, Mabel meditates on her dwindling love for her husband, Allen. She suspects that he is having an affair with a neighbor woman, Patricia. Patricia's new baby looks just like her husband, and the infant's name, Alexander, is the final clue that she needs: "Nobody in her family named Alexander" (129). The story climaxes when Patricia asks Mabel to babysit Alexander after church. Mabel agrees, though she burns with rage at the indignity of having to look after the baby who may be her husband's illegitimate son. Mabel tries hard to keep it together, but she slowly loses her battle to maintain her composure. The baby screams, and Mabel goes to comfort him. She finds the screaming causes her to lose a bit of her vision, and before she knows it, she has dropped him on the floor. The renewed screaming of the injured infant causes Mabel more pain—"in Mabel's head the wail becomes a choir of voices. Images. The deer. Mr. Todd. Patricia. . . . Screeches of hate. Accusation. She wants to go away. Into the television forever. She wants to be nice forever" (137).

Overcome by grief, Mabel throws Alexander across the room. When the baby hits the wall and stops screaming, she is finally at peace, and her "whole mind is flooded with God's Holy Light" (137). She picks the lifeless Alexander up and rocks him. In her new fantasy, she imagines that the little baby belongs to her and Allen. She wants to name the infant Elroy after her father. At the end of the story, we have glimpses of Mabel in handcuffs, in an ambulance, calling out for her imaginary Elroy, even as the narrator asks us to "sing a song" for her (139).

### "This Far; Or, a Body in Motion"

Written in the second person, Kenan seems to be writing *to* Booker T. Washington, who started as a houseboy for General Ruffner in 1867—"a post-Emancipation slave is more accurate" (140). The narrator acknowledges that Washington has "been in constant motion" since his birth, "as if from the first day you understood the Newtonian axiom: A body in motion tends to stay in motion" (141). In the story, Washington visits Tims Creek a month before his death, in November 1915, to visit Elihu and Tabitha McElwaine, old friends from more than thirty years ago. Tabitha has solicited Washington to come to Tims Creek because she is the "mistress of the colored school" (147), which is having its inauguration. At first, Washington finds himself compelled to attend because of his memory of Tabitha and the dim hope that she has not yet married, but, more important, what keeps him moving is the shadowy feeling that he may fail at something and so must try harder to never stop.

At the packed inauguration for the school, Washington delivers his trademark oratory. "Your act is a magic show. Mesmerizing. Spellbinding. You start out somewhat folksy, down-home—without, of course, losing your magisterial air" (151). And yet, the narrator asks Washington, "As you step down to the cheers and palpitating applause and seek your chair, do you think of your critics and question how far work work work work work will really take these people? Work worked for you because you were ruthless, conniving, unscrupulous, untiring, and always brilliant. Without a doubt you know this. How many Negro men and women did you trample just to hold on? Just to hold on? It seems the more powerful the Machine becomes, the harder it is to remember your original goals" (151–152).

The narrator then asks Washington to consider the relationship between Tabitha and Elihu's romance and Washington's constant drive to travel and work; "they changed your view of the possibilities for Negroes. You had dreamt of it, read of it, of Negroes who had something other than hunger and poverty and debts. . . . What amazing world did they come from?" (153). Washington is stunned that he admires something he cannot—may never—own: happiness, peace.

At dinner, Elihu's son challenges Washington over his accommodation to white businessmen. "Why must we wait," he asks Washington, and then pointedly critiques his patience for white culture: "Time alone won't solve all our problems" (157–158). When Washington tries to engage Elihu, he finds the old man just as prickly as his son. Though Elihu won't criticize Washington openly, he does believe that there is truth in what Washington's critics assert. He astonishes Washington by telling him he not only knew Frederick Douglass but saved his life one time. Hearing the story, the narrator notes, "you are a young boy again, amazed by the possibilities of the world" (161). The story ends with the narrator noting that Washington will die soon and that he must be tired. But the question that remains long after his death, even in the wake of his time on earth, even into the late twentieth century, is what was going on inside Washington's head when he finally stopped his work, when he finally lay down to die: "does your illusion hold? . . . you will keep moving moving moving moving moving to finish to finish to finish—what? Do you know?" (162).

**"Run, Mourner, Run"**

Kenan's story is about Dean Williams; when we first meet him, he is swinging on the same tire swing his daddy put up when Dean was five years old. Now twenty-three, Dean still sits on the same swing like a little boy waiting to be called in to supper by his mama. Dean's mind drifts back to March, when Percy Terrell picked him up to ask him for a favor. Until that day, the two men had never had much to do with each other: Dean was only "poor white trash: a sweet-faced, dark-haired faggot with a broken-down Ford Torino, living with his chain-smoking mama in a damn-near condemned house they didn't even own" (166), while Percy was one of the big wigs in Tims Creek. Percy asked Dean to seduce Raymond Brown, who owned some land that the older man needed.

Thinking about the proposition made Dean dizzy, especially the idea of "sex with a black man" (167), but the promise of a promotion to foreman at the local plant and the six-thousand-dollar raise that came with it was almost too much to turn down. The next day, at McTarr's Grocery, Dean found Raymond, and the two discussed cars. A few days later, Dean went to "The Jack Rabbit" in Raleigh, the bar that Percy told him Raymond frequented, and the young man made his move. Infatuated with Dean, Raymond took the young man to his old homestead on the very land that Percy lusted after; as they undressed and made love "underneath a quilt made by Ray's great-grandmother" (177), Dean "felt certain he heard the voices of old black men and old black women screaming for his death, his blood, for him to be strung up on a Judas tree" (177).

One night, Dean and Raymond were awakened at the homestead by a group of white men who took pictures of them in bed; the scene was full of sounds that hurt Dean to hear, "the sound of dogs panting: claws on wooden floors: the boys mumbling under their breath; fucking queers, fucking faggots" (179). When Percy mussed Dean's hair and congratulated him on a job well done, Dean noted Ray's face in a "configuration of anger, loathing, coldness, disdain, recognition, as though he suddenly realized he had been in bed with a cottonmouth moccasin or a stinking dog" (181). Raymond angrily asked Percy to leave and then demanded Dean go as well. Now, struck by the enormity of what he has done, Dean wants only to be held by Raymond, but he is rejected again and again. Leaving the house, Dean tries "to dredge up every nigger, junglebunny, cocksucking, motherfucking, sambo insult he could muster; he wanted to relearn hate, fiery, blunt, brutal" (183).

As the weeks go by, Dean is not rewarded by Terrell. The young man's mother gets sick several times, and bills pile up. Dean finally decides to go to Terrell's store and ask him in person when he will be promoted. But Percy pretends he doesn't understand what Dean is talking about. When Dean reaches out to the man to plead for mercy, Percy responds, "Don't you ever lay a hand on me again, faggot" (186). Percy's boys beat Dean viciously and drop a twenty-dollar bill at his feet. But it is his emotional wounds that Dean feels will never heal. In a final twist of the knife, Raymond's wife stops her car to help Dean after he has dropped his groceries on the ground. Giving him a ride home, she asks Dean if he's saved. Dean explains he is not, and when Mrs. Brown offers him advice, Dean meekly says, "Some things you just let happen." "My husband always says that," she responds. "Now ain't that funny" (190). Back home by the tire swing with his momma calling him for supper, Dean waits for the world to end; lost in an illusion of childhood memories and nursery rhymes, he waits, hoping someday to believe in childish fantasies again.

**"What Are Days?"**

In the opening scene of this story, Kenan juxtaposes a youthful, naked young man asleep on the bed with Lena, "a mature woman of experience. A ripened woman." She wakes the sleeping man by piercing his naked buttocks with the pin side of her brooch. Backing up to the previous Friday, the same day the boy came to visit her, Kenan tells us that Lena had gone to see her husband's gravesite. Thurston "Cannonball" Walker, like Lena, had been born in Tims Creek, but she decided to inter him in Newark because neither of them had family in the town anymore. A veteran of several wars, Thurston had been beloved by men more than women; "he seemed to be always surrounded by men and boys and cigar smoke and uproarious laughter" (195). Her pilgrimage to his gravesite happened to coincide with her fifty-first birthday.

On her way back from the store, Lena encountered some young men; when she told them it was her birthday, they made a grand show of wishing her a happy day. One young man, Shang, asked her if he could deliver a birthday present to her in person, around eight o'clock that night. When she agreed, he blew her a kiss, and the sudden titillation of a new man thrilled her: "not a boyhood 'I love you, Mom' kiss, no; nor a 'You nice *older* woman, let me be polite and gallant' kiss, uh-uh; not a kiss of insincerity and lies, which she felt confident she could divine . . . this was one of those young-boy kisses that spoke of tongues and hot juices and getting naked" (199). Shang's interest in her fascinated Lena and shook her out of her boredom and meaningless routines—going to work, cleaning the house, working to make everything proper. "Why? For whom did she keep going going going? If she allowed herself to stop and wonder she would surely be overwhelmed by the emptiness. Better to fool herself into thinking her days were so full" (203).

When Shang arrived with chocolates and flowers, Lena was shocked that he kissed her full on the mouth; he stayed the weekend with her. They made love and spent an entire day in bed just spending time together. Though the difference in their ages made Lena uncomfortable, she found pleasure in being around the nineteen-year-old boy. He claimed to not care about the generational differences, but Lena still wondered "how could he, a nineteen-year-old child, look at a fifty-one-year-old woman and see her? See her diminishing menstrual cramps, her sore feet, back pains, and tired legs. . . . How could he, a young kid, know lust in the presence of someone surely as old as his mother? Or older?" (207). When Shang doesn't come back to see her for over two weeks, Lena goes crazy with fear. But her fear quickly turns to anger, and she sets out to find him.

With the Al Green song "Let's Stay Together" burning in her ears, Lena remembers life with Cannonball and how little he valued her; he was always more concerned with his friends and poker games. When Lena arrives at Shang's house, the boy who answers to that name looks nothing like her young lover from before. She retreats in confusion and panic. At home, she runs to the record player and tries to throw it out the window, but she trips and falls, destroying the machine. Lost in a sea of memories of what Shang did for her—"like the Tin Man, she felt remade, bit by bit, bite by bite" (217)—Lena lets the idea of him go. Freeing herself from "the *idea* of Shang" liberates the woman from her soulless life. In a final act of reclamation, she sits in Cannonball's "mammoth recliner" and reaches for a cigarette (219).

### "Ragnarök! The Day the Gods Die"

Kenan weaves two narratives into this story—the first a sermon delivered at the funeral of "Sister Louise Tate" and the second, written in italics and parentheses, containing the memories and confessions of the preacher who speaks throughout the piece. Though his eulogy is a conventional message delivered to mourners, the preacher has thoughts that are anything but holy. Even as the preacher praises Louise's soul, his memories of her are all carnal: "I see her sitting on the bed that way with her back arched just like a cat and her titties just as pert and them nipples just as hard as dimes" (220). While he preaches, the man can't help recalling the details of his lustful thoughts, both for his wife, Sarah, and for other women, and the sting of his son's rebuke when he discovered his father's sexual escapades with Louise.

Lost in his thoughts about the good man he was supposed to be, the preacher prays not to God but to Louise, to rescue him, to take him home, to rock him like a sweet baby. "Louise, I lived for those meetings, those quick moments of sweet breath, in motel rooms. . . . You lie before me, baby girl, it's hard to believe. You're cold, child. I wish I could warm you" (228–230); he speaks directly to the woman he is eulogizing. Turning from Louise's cold body, the preacher then speaks to the Lord; he asks why "you've taken them both and left me to find out what I've been preaching all these years, left me to come at it face to face" (231–232). Staring at his life and his shame, all the preacher can do is rely on grace, but he finds it no comfort. Even as he speaks of the power of grace to his flock, the man knows "I shall never be purified" (233). The story ends with the preacher hopelessly lost in the ambivalence of his shame and grief—"What kind of fool am I who'd rather deny God than face Him? Do I hear wings? Do they come or do they go? Or is it just the sound of the wind?" (234).

**"Tell Me, Tell Me"**

Kenan's story starts with a phone call involving two older women, Ida McTyre Perry and her friend, Bela. Ida has called Bela because she believes a black boy has broken into her house, and she wants Bela to send help. Bela is skeptical because two weeks prior to the call, Ida had crashed her car—with Ida in it—because she believed she had seen the same boy in the middle of the road—but that was not the first time she had seen the boy. His specter has haunted her for years. Once, when Ida was having lunch at the Old Plantation Inn, "a restaurant oozing quaintness and doilied charm" (246), she looked out the window during a rainstorm and saw him across the street. Staring right at her, the boy's eyes bore in her memory: "His head had that African shape: too large for his thin frame and shaped like a peanut" (247). Their staring game made Ida angry, and when she turned for a moment and then again looked for the boy, he had disappeared. She has seen the boy many times but almost doesn't mark the occasions. He is virtually forgettable, but she remembers specifically that one time when she was in her garden and saw him walking along the edge, she told him to get off her property. When the boy finally turned to her, "his look was full of accusation" (248).

Kenan shifts his narrative from the memories of Ida's interactions with the ghostly boy to her memories of life with her husband, to her pride in her son, to the birth of her grandson, and to one specific moment when she was diagnosed with a spot on her uterus during a routine X-ray. She recalls Joe Abner, her servant, who wandered in one evening to find her slumped over her knitting. Believing she was dead, Joe screamed in terror, and Ida woke up. At first she was upset with him, but she relented, thinking, "he has . . . character, yes, that's it, *character.* So many of them don't, these days. The way he brings me things from his wife's garden, the way he treats me respectfully" (253). Still, she realized that, while Joe had worked for her for twenty-five years, she knew virtually nothing about him; he was "a grand and impenetrable mystery" (253). In fact, neither Ida nor her husband, Judge Theodore S. Perry, really desired to know anything about African Americans, even though they considered themselves to be good, racially tolerant white southerners.

Because of her brush with illness and the false alarm of the X-ray—the spot turned out to be merely a benign infection—Ida has kept her mysterious encounters with the vision of the boy to herself. She fears someone will think her senile. Finally, lost in a fog of her own memories, illusions, and fantasies, she recalls a moment on Emerald Isle in August 1937 when her then-beau, Butch Perry, took her to a secluded spot to fool around. Their lovemaking was interrupted by a young black boy who stumbled onto the two lovers in the middle of intercourse. The child ran away but was quickly tracked down by Butch, who viciously kicked and beat him before throwing him deep into the ocean. As Butch came back to the beach, Ida "forces herself to smile: no, not forces: wills, creates, manufactures a smile: it is real, her smile, not fake: he is just a bad boy, her Butch: tsk, tsk. . . . Just a nigger: Just a nigger" (267–268). Deep within her soul, Ida finds the "images locked away. . . . But some things you forget to remain innocent. . . . Ida had not cared to remember; not to remain innocent, not to remain free, not to spare herself worry, but because she simply did not care" (268). Kenan switches back to the present time: the boy stands at the foot of Ida's bed, and though she runs from the room, down the stairs, out of the house, and into the night, she knows she will never escape: "All are guilty, none is free" (269).

### "Let the Dead Bury Their Dead"

Kenan's final story—and the eponymous piece of the collection—is a much longer and more complicated piece than the ones that precede it. The full title is "Let the Dead Bury Their Dead; Being the Annotated Oral History of the Former Maroon Society Called Snatchit and then Tearshirt and later the Town of Tims Creek, North Carolina [circa 1854–1985]." It is supposedly written by the "Right Reverend James Malachai Greene," the same minister who appeared in Kenan's *A Visitation of Spirits,* and the framing device of the book is that the story has been "abridged and edited, with an introduction by Reginald Gregory Kain," a clear stand-in for Randall G. Kenan. In many ways, the story deepens the narrative of *Visitation* by imagining the lives of central characters beyond the ending of that book and also by revisiting the world of "darkness" into which Horace crosses during the final chapters of the novel.

In the introduction, Kain-as-Kenan tells us that Jimmy Greene died in a car accident in 1998 just as he was returning from a conference in Atlanta. In addition to being the town's minister, Jimmy was also its secret historian, "quietly chronicling the Tims Creek of past and present, of public and private, of mythic and real, of virtue and vice" (277). His papers, which Kain tells us are housed at "the Southern Historical Collection in Chapel Hill, North Carolina, have not been fully catalogued, but the complete works are estimated to exceed over 500,000 words" (279). Kain tells us that the story that follows is the result of a conversation between two familiar characters from *Visitation:* Ezekiel (Zeke) Thomas Cross and Ruth David Cross. Weaving in autobiography, folklore, fiction, letters, and "discourses on natural history" (280), Kain reminds the reader of his own connection with Kenan (the introduction is written in 2000 from Brooklyn, New York and the acknowledgments section thanks Sarah Lawrence College for providing funding for Kain to visit Tims Creek) and his own aesthetic/ethos throughout his fiction.

Zeke's voice begins the story; he tells of the origins of Tims Creek, how it was first known as Snatchit and later as Tearshirt: "won't see that in none of them textbooks they give you up in that University," he explains (283). The town was a "maroon society" for slaves who had escaped their bondage and built a village deep in the swamps "so as the white folks couldn't find them." Zeke tries to explain the significance of a swell of earth in Tims Creek, offering competing explanations for its existence, including an Indian burial ground and the earth mourning for the death of its citizens. He is frequently interrupted in his narrative by Ruth, who challenges him on the veracity of his claims, and by the annotations of Greene and Kain, who draw upon both real and imaginary texts to refute or complicate Zeke's telling of the town's history (one notable false text is a short-story collection by Randall Kenan himself, *Go Curse Your God, Boy, and Die: Stories* [286n]). "Will you let me tell my story," Zeke demands through all Ruth's interruptions.

In one narrative of the earth's swell, Zeke explains, there was an old slave who was buried with a book of intense magic/spiritual power. The townsfolk heard the book was actually a treasure map, and they went to dig up the slave's grave, only to find the coffin empty. When old Mose Pickett appeared to confirm the gravesite, the men ran in terror: Mose had been buried a week ago. According to Zeke, that buried slave was named Pharaoh, and he was known throughout that territory because he had been a powerful presence. During his time with the Waccamaw Indians, Pharaoh learned "something powerful from the . . . medicine man" (297). When his master got tired of Pharaoh's shenanigans, he sold him to the Crosses: "they was *the* family in North Carolina in them days." Though Ruth contests Zeke's story about Pharaoh's coming to the Crosses—she has heard a story that he was won in a card game—they both agree that the enslaved man began to slowly work his way into the power structure of the Cross family. At one point, folks "say he got so much power over Cross he [Pharaoh] could give orders to white overseers" (300). Zeke explains that, when Pharaoh had built up enough power, the slave engineered a revolt that burned the Crosses' plantation house to the ground and resulted in the death of eight white overseers, including the Crosses' son, Owen. Pharaoh escaped shortly after the fire and set up residence in the place that is now called Tims Creek, a swampy site that was difficult to navigate and hides him from the white men hunting him.

The town continued to grow, as did Pharaoh's importance in the community. He was both a town leader and a kind of shaman for his people. In a flashback, Greene offers a section from the diary of Cross's wife, Sarah. In it, we learn that the lady feared for her life and believed Pharaoh, whom she called Menes, to be the devil himself. One night, she dreamed the slave entered her room "*Naked* but for a white cloth about *His Loins & Forced Himself upon me*, but He did not *Disturb My Virtue*. He shackled me instead and Forced me to do *labor*" (310). Breaking back to Zeke's narrative, the man recounts the entrance of a mysterious "preacher" in the town. The preacher's grip over the citizens of the town was powerful, too; he also performed miracles, such as curing an old man of his blindness. The preacher's hold over the town was a direct affront to Pharaoh's; "by and by, he had folk damn near worshipping him," Zeke explains.

Things in the town started to become strange: a girl began to lose her mind and tried to make love to a persimmon tree; a beautiful boy started acting like a dog and fornicating with goats and hogs; and a seven-year-old boy "turned into a devil . . . they finally found him in the creek, his head turned all the way around and naked" (317–318). The gossip in the town was that the victims of these afflictions were the sexual partners of the preacherman. One day, the preacher preached a sermon against Pharaoh and told his congregation that God had told him in a dream to dig up Pharaoh's body, for there was a secret key to a great treasure. Here, the narrative breaks again to a letter from Phineas Cross to his English lover, Nigel; Phineas describes his stumbling upon the colony of Menes/Pharaoh and how the slave pardoned him from his transgression on his land. Pharaoh explained to Phineas that he was being pardoned for the kindness Phineas had shown to his people, but Menes/Pharaoh warned him never to utter a word about their meeting to anyone.

Again, the story breaks to Zeke as he explains what happens when they tried to dig up Pharaoh: everyone dead in the town rose up, "clawing out of their graves. Like Lazarus" (327). They ran through the town, causing havoc, righting personal wrongs and taking revenge on those who had hurt them in life. The townsfolk ran for safety to the church, but they found it full of adders. When they heard the preacher's voice outside the church door telling them to have faith, they opened it, but he was not there. The townsfolk decided to make a break for it, but they found the preacher waiting with an army of the dead—the zombie corpses were "all sorts of evil creatures . . . wolves walking on they hind legs, buzzards eating people alive, red demons with bats' wings" (331). Suddenly, out of nowhere, Pharaoh appeared riding a great bull; he lopped off the preacher's head with a sword in one mighty blow. When Pharaoh left, fire rained down from the sky, and the wicked were burned for days on end. All that was left is the mound of dirt that was still visible to the town.

According to Zeke, the only survivors of the inferno were an old woman and a boy named Elihu McElwaine (the father of the old Elihu from Kenan's earlier story "This Far"). Starting over and giving the town a new name, Tims Creek, Elihu creates a world of both black and white citizens: "See, ole Elihu had laid claim to some land the Crosses figured they owned; but it was Malcolm Terrell finally swindled both of them out of that land. And it was Elihu McElwaine who kilt Malcolm Terrell. And his son Percy kilt Elihu in revenge. But that's another story" (333). Kenan's final story ends with Ruth contesting the whole plot of Zeke's story, especially his narrative about Elihu. From when she was a little girl, she remembers Elihu and Tabitha, the children of Elihu and his wife, who came from Mississippi, not from surviving the fire of the damned. They didn't inherit the earth; they "bought some swampy back land from ole Thomas Cross, who got it from the white Cross family back in the 1860s. Drained it, made it workable. Then, come the Depression, he had to sell it to Malcolm Terrell" (334). She challenges Zeke, too, on the story of the mound; she had heard it was caused by a meteor striking the earth. When Ruth rebukes Zeke for his lies, the man shoots back, "All I know is what my granddaddy told me, and boy, that was like I told you, word for word, near bout. Near bout."

**Sorrow Songs: Blues and the Soul of Mourning**

Like *Visitation, LTDBTD* works through the lens of tragedy to explicate the way in which frustrations over identity can ultimately trap characters in a cycle of endless suffering. Kenan borrows heavily from both the central themes, ethos, and structure of the blues to work through the tragedy of his characters. In speaking about his story "The Strange and Tragic Ballad of Mabel Pearsall," Kenan said:

> So the repetition-the dum, dum, dum; the Mabel, Mabel, Mabel—the quick images, even the structure of the whole story, I was hoping to get to a blues ballad. And when I say blues, I mean Muddy Waters blues, Bessie Smith blues, my-house-burned-down-and-I-ain't-got-nowhere-to-live blues. That's why I call it "The Strange and Tragic Ballad of Mabel Pearsall." I

> don't know if it worked entirely on that level. It's difficult, but I'm very interested in that. One of my very favorite writers, Anthony Burgess, is interesting because he keeps saying you can't write prose like music. Music appeals directly to the emotions. Music is essentially mathematical, uses too different a logic, doesn't work on the same chromatic scale. But he keeps trying it. . . . It's an urge I think we share. All writers really want to be singers. "The Strange and Tragic Ballad of Mabel Pearsall" was the first time I admitted that. . . . Anyway, that was the basic idea behind the story.[4]

In the story, Kenan presents his reader with snippets of images—"Mabel in bed. Mabel at night. Mabel can't sleep" (129)—that work to set a tone of repetitive sorrow. In the blues tradition, lyrics are often repeated in order that they may show a progressive emphasis on the cycle of despair the singer articulates. Similarly, Mabel's life is a progression of repetitive events that lead to a feeling of claustrophobic sadness. The woman does the same ritual every single day; she tries hard to do the right thing. But Mabel is never allowed to grow or become the person she wants to be; she is trapped. Her circular movement working toward no satisfying conclusion is echoed by Kenan's prose.

Kenan also presents sections of songs throughout "The Strange and Tragic Ballad of Mabel Pearsall," but many of them are not actual blues lyrics but rather the lyrics to lullabies and gospel songs. The tragedy that befalls Mabel —her husband's possible affair and impregnation of Patricia—complicates the simplicity of lullabies like "Hush little baby, don't you cry" (138) or "Go to sleepy, little baby / Mama and Papa both gone away, / Left nobody but the baby" (135). Both sets of lyrics attempt to quiet the sorrow of the child through song, but the lyrics recognize abandonment as the very sadness the singer is trying to alleviate. Kenan also uses the trope of "sleep" to connect with death; he positions the chorus to "Sail Away, Ladies"—"Ain't no reason to sit and cry / You'll be an angel, by and by"(126)—as the ultimate sleep, an end to all sadness and sorrow. And the final lyric of the story asks for a decorated coffin so that the singer might "look pretty as I ride along" (138) to her funeral. By referencing both the ethos and the actual structure of the blues as well as gospel and popular music, Kenan renegotiates his story into a kind of sorrow song and suggests that all songs steeped in the African American tradition carry with them, at base, an articulation of despair.

Lyrics carry a similar weight of sorrow in "Run, Mourner, Run," and, as in "The Strange and Tragic Ballad of Mabel Pearsall," much of the sadness tied to their meanings comes from the gap between childlike articulations of simplicity and the complicated truth of the adult world. Dean Williams, the central protagonist, is a young man without a mature understanding of social or cultural interactions. He is naïve in both his personal and his sexual exchanges. Part of his naïveté comes because he is so marginalized within the community, both as poor white trash and as a gay man in a small southern town: "In Percy's eyes Dean was nothing more than poor white trash: a sweet-faced, dark-haired faggot" (166). Percy takes advantage of Dean's naïveté to manipulate him into blackmailing Raymond. When the scheme works, however, Percy does not hold up his end of the deal, and Dean is left with nothing. Throughout the story, Kenan peppers in direct quotations from nursery rhymes and childish sayings that work to both comment on Dean's childish view of the world and suggest the darkness lurking behind the stories we tell young people.

Toward the end of the story, a disillusioned Dean is barely able to scrape by and pay his mother's medical bills. In a final twist of fate, he finds himself in the car with the wife of the very man he blackmailed. Kenan inserts several rhymes that comment on the irony of Dean's situation and also articulate the sorrow of the young man's disillusion: "Moses supposes his toeses are roses, / But Moses supposes erroneously" (188), and "If all the world was apple pie / And all the sea was ink, / And all the trees were bread and cheese, / What would we have to drink?" (190). Beyond being comforting rhymes that express Dean's childlike view of the world around him, these poems express the dark truth that lurks behind imaginative fantasy. Supposing erroneously is Dean's very hamartia, and his childish fantasy of transactional intimacy ultimately authors his tragedy. Dean gets nothing he imagines will come to him, and he is left alone and hurt. The vulnerability of childish wishes only exposes places that men like Percy can exploit, and the imaginative language of nursery rhymes morphs into a song of mourning.

In "What Are Days," Lena is haunted by a specific song, Al Green's "Let's Stay Together." It is the song that is playing when Shang comes to see her, and it is that song that stays with her throughout the story. For Lena, Al Green is "the slow night music, love music, sex music" (192). It is the single that her young lover plays repeatedly, and the words and music together burn in her memory about the liberating sexual experience she has that weekend. While she explores the young man's body, it is "Al Green's phrasing [that] had been indelibly seared across her brain, between her legs, on her breast" (210). Finally, Lena is unable to untangle the song from the experience: "That brass, that old organ music, Al's high tenor. Damn. She couldn't think of one without the other. Shang and the song. The slow groove, she was certain, had affected the beat of her heart" (210).

But if the song works as an anthem of liberation, it also does double work through its lyrics. Al Green's music might be "sex music," but, at its heart, "Let's Stay Together" is a song about fidelity and commitment. In a way, the lyrics articulate the tragedy of Lena's existence with her verbally abusive husband, Cannonball, and they help Lena see the sorrow of her boring existence. Shang and Cannonball are present in Al Green's lyrics in various ways. While Shang might be representative of Green's celebration of the potential for sexual empowerment—"Cause you make me feel brand neeewwww" (218)—Lena must surely be reminded of her husband, Cannonball, with the chorus "Let's stay together." For the entirety of her marriage, Lena stayed true and faithful to Cannonball, even though he clearly loved poker and his friends more than her. In a flashback scene where Lena begs her husband to stop the card game so she can get some sleep, Cannonball roars, "Bitch, just shut the fuck up. . . . This is my house, goddammit. My house" (211). That night, Lena realizes that, though they might "turn around and make up" as Al Green offers in his song, "even then she would still be alone" (212). A song about sexual liberation becomes a blues riff. Only through the lens of the song does Lena see the sorrow of her life. She stumbles over the chair going to throw the record player out the window, but, with the needle pulled from Al Green's repetitive articulation of her sorrow, she becomes a changed woman. No longer drowning in the heart of her sorrow song, Lena is altered; she rejects sorrow for joy: "Laughing, she walked about the house regally. Laughing, she changed the funky bedsheets. . . . Laughing, she took a fat steak from the deep freeze. . . . Lena snickered at her old existence" (219). Free from the broken record of her own internal blues, Lena rejects sorrow for joy and reclaims what is hers when she sits "down in Cannonball's mammoth recliner."

### Transgressive Intimacies and the Power of Sexual Identity

Lena's story in "What Are Days" is one of the few instances in Kenan's collection where sexual awakening leads to liberation; though Lena feels trapped at first by her obsession with Shang, she ultimately finds his opening of her perspective to be a healthy space of potential empowerment: "she watched the *idea* of Shang, like a bird released from captivity, unfold wings and take flight" (219). However, many of the stories in *LTDBTD* use sexuality as a means through which characters become trapped; depending on the character and his or her circumstances, sexuality can either be a means through which to express a healthy identity or a barb that snares the character in a cycle of endless and meaningless suffering. Similarly, the manufacturing of intimacies—not necessarily sexual—create spaces throughout the text where Kenan suggests real communication can happen. Instances of intimacy allow the potential for Kenan's characters to liberate and empower themselves, even as the closeness he describes crosses all kinds of axes of generations, ethnicities, regions, nationalities, and gender.

The potential for empowerment is present in "The Foundations of the Earth," when Maggie puts away her hatred and arrogance and tries to understand Gabriel and Edward's relationship. She has no context for the intimacies shared between men, especially sexual intimacy, and at first she rejects the value of their love. But gradually Maggie lets go of her judgment and begins to ask the questions that will help her understand who her grandson was. At one point in the story, Maggie asks Gabriel, "But don't you *want* to be normal?"; the young man responds, "I *am*. Normal" (64). Maggie's ability both to ask the hard questions and to be able to hear their answers, to see Gabriel's position and perspective, makes the intimacy she shares with him a source of empowerment. By the end of the story, her understanding of her dead grandson's identity opens Maggie up to evolve and grow: "Now he was gone. And now she had come to terms with this news of his being 'gay,' as the world called what she had been taught was an unholy abomination. . . . I should have known better. I must learn better" (69). Understanding the validity of Gabriel and Edward's love leads to Maggie's rejection of her judgmental arrogance and allows her to become truly free. "How strange that at seventy, when she had all the laws and rules down pat, she would have to begin again, to learn" (72), Kenan writes, but it is Maggie's adaptability and her willingness to grow that open up a space for a cross-racial/cross-generational intimacy and finally lead to her potential for empowerment and liberation.

Cross-generational/cross-ethnic intimacies also offer a source of empowerment in "Things of This World"; John Edgar Stokes tends to an injured stranger, Chi, who, according to the man, is "a Chinaman. Just like he had seen on TV. Look at them eyes, he thought. Just as slanted as a cat's" (26). Though the two men share nothing in common, Stokes shares his food and space with him; Stokes asks nothing in return from Chi. And gradually the two men become close in a way that confounds the town. Kenan clearly suggests that Chi is a kind of angel for Stokes, just as Gabriel—with his name check of an actual saint and angel—performs a kind of ministering to Maggie. Stokes requires nothing of Chi and never asks the man to explain himself. The reward for their open intimacy is the granting of Stokes's final wish—to die on his own terms. In both "Things of This World" and "The Foundations of the Earth," the crossing of the axes of generation and race/ethnicity provides a useful and fruitful terrain for characters to grow.

Kenan also provides instances throughout *LTDBTD* where the potential for cross-generational/cross-racial intimacies is foreclosed and the inability of characters to speak across their perspectives provides a kind of tragic breakdown in the process of true liberation. In "Clarence and the Dead," for example, the relationship between the four-year-old Clarence and the middle-aged

Ellsworth is something the town cannot tolerate: "Nothing like talk of crimes against nature gets people all riled up and speculating and conjecturing and postulating the way they did when word got out about Ellsworth Batts's 'unnatural affection' for Clarence Pickett" (19). Because Clarence can supposedly speak to the dead, his channeling of Ellsworth's wife causes the older man to "court" him; the folks of Tims Creek see their relationship as "depraved intentions for young and tender boys" (19). Here, the town forecloses the possibility for intimacy between a man and a boy, not simply because of its cross-generational nature but also because of the specter of same-sex intimacy. Kenan is quick to point out that it is the townspeople's failure of imagination that leads to their inability to connect with Clarence or the world of the spirit. When Batts kills himself by jumping off the bridge, Clarence dies soon after. And the town refuses to exercise its imagination: "We figured there was more to it than that, something our imaginations were too timid to draw up, something to do with living and dying that we, so wound up in harvesting corn, cleaning house, minding chickenpox, building houses, getting our hair done, getting our cars fixed, getting good loving, fishing, drinking, sleeping, and minding other people's business, really didn't care about or have time and space to know. Why mess in such matters—matters we really didn't believe in in the first place, and of which the memory grows dimmer every time the sun sets" (22).

The ability to imagine another's perspective leads to both the potential for intimacy and the ability to grow. Without imagination, characters remain stuck in *LTDBTD,* wanting to reach out and touch someone, like Thad at the end of "The Origin of Whales," but ultimately drawing back inward, their open hand turning into an image of violent isolationism, a "balled . . . fist" (87).

Tims Creek is a closed space, a bordered land that forbids certain kinds of transgressions. Tucker notes that "the community has attributed its survival to the rigid maintenance of patriarchal family structures, stable racial identities, and normative sexual desires. Yet, as Kenan is intent on showing, such control—often imaged in tropes of spatiality—is unrealistic, unworkable, and only serves to underscore the permeability of all borders, whether communal, bodily, or psychic."[5] When the community feels itself threatened by a potential transgression, it entrenches the borders between generations, races, and genders. A foreclosure of intimacy—no matter how it is authored—always results in the frustration of identity in *LTDBTD;* frequently, the lack of intimacy draws characters inside their own heads, where the characters torture themselves endlessly in a cycle of unsatisfying and meaningless suffering. Nowhere is the failure of imaginative intimacy more clearly connected to a cycle of suffering than in the story "Cornsilk." The main character of the story feels trapped by his love for his half-sister, Jamonica, or, more specifically, the memory of his physical expression of their lust. He spends the opening sections of the story detailing the beauty of Jamonica's body and the way in which the memory of his sexual escapades have become almost sacred texts to recite and celebrate. At the very point of orgasm, the narrator says, "We make a joyful noise unto the Lord, a raucous noise, an unholy song of heat and lust to an unholy Lord. Lord, Lord, Lord" (89).

But the narrator's obsessive celebration of the memory of Jamonica's body and their sexual liberation is tinged with the sorrow of her absence. She rejects him and their love and leaves the narrator with nothing on which to build the meaning of his existence. Foreclosing their space of intimacy because it is "wrong" (113), Jamonica rejects a liberated existence for herself and her brother. The narrator gets trapped in an endless cycle of meaningless sexual adventures that never satisfy him: "I've tried the escort services. Pathetic. These women, I mean. . . . Nothing like Jamonica . . . for it is a trade to them, serving up fantasy. I never tell them they are to be my sister" (95). And Jamonica, too, "is trapped, you see. She fell in love. She married. But it's not a happy tale. . . . I visited her last month but I didn't see her. Not the woman I smuggled in my dorm room . . . her body now misshapen from multiple births" (109). The only thing the two siblings have left is the memory of what they once shared, the moment in which they celebrated their intimacy despite, or maybe because of, its transgressive nature, its violation of a taboo. In conversation with Hunt, Kenan noted, "I didn't want the earth to open and scoop Aaron back down into it. But I realized that even if incest isn't a taboo, and even if this is all superstition and mumbo jumbo, that because of the environment in which he grew up, and because of what his root beliefs are, he was going to feel this way about himself. And that ultimately is where the psychological damage comes in."[6]

And, finally, in "Ragnarök! The Day the Gods Die," the preacher-narrator traps himself within a similar cell of suffering because of his love for Louise, the woman he eulogizes. He mourns for her loss inwardly, but the mourning takes on a feeling of double-speak because he also mourns his inability to celebrate his love for a woman he did not marry. Like "Cornsilk," "Ragnarök!" investigates the complications of a love that isn't allowed to exist in the small religious community of Tims Creek, and the disconnection between what the narrator feels physically and what he must project socially is represented by two competing narratives: his eulogy, told in straight prose, and his inward dialogue/memory, literally hemmed in by parentheses and "whispered" in italics. The gaps between what the preacher thinks and what he says are stark; he might be speaking about grace and sanctity, but inside, his thoughts are carnal:

"I am not in despair to see her body there still before me. . . . Sweet sweet beloved hot pussy" (221).

Beyond causing frustration in the preacher's personal life—his son rejects him, and his wife grows distant—the lusting after Louise causes him to question the very foundation of his place in the church and the town. How is he supposed to be the authority on matters of the heart when he is a victim of his own physical desires? "What else can I say," he confesses. "The Lord's army is in trouble cause the Devil's arsenal is mighty, mighty sweet. I stand as a witness" (223). In the end, his inability to reconcile his love for Louise with his position in the town causes him to live out a fractured and meaningless identity. He cannot minister to his congregation because he is impure, and he cannot understand the grace given to sinners because he cannot offer that same grace to himself. His denial of the love of Louise forecloses a space for him to grow into a person of value; instead, he becomes "the living dead denied the grave. No harbor. No nipple to suckle, no buttock to caress. I was a fool who lived by grace and I abused grace, I used grace like a whore. . . . Grace once had wings, but I rode it unto death" (233). Denying opportunities for transgressive or even trans-social intimacies always leads to the frustration of identity in *LTDBTD* and authors many of the tragedies of the characters of Tims Creek.

**The Power of the Porch: Adjudicating Truth and Fantasy**

In her book *The Power of the Porch: The Storyteller's Craft in Zora Neale Hurston, Gloria Naylor, and Randall Kenan,* Trudier Harris works through the tradition of "porch talk" in African American literature as a means of both entertainment—telling stories—and community building.[7] In *Let the Dead Bury Their Dead,* Randall Kenan uses the porch as a crucial site in which what is true and what is false gets adjudicated amid various constituencies and audiences. This contestation of facts and fantasy is highly interactive and, in many cases, performative and comes to constitute the basis for a variety of ways in which the town speaks to itself about itself. More important, the performance of truth-talk on the porch offers a more coherent belief structure for the folks of the town than the church or the family gives on its own.

The final story of Kenan's collection, the titular "Let the Dead Bury Their Dead," is a perfect example of the way in which fact and fantasy get adjudicated by competing voices. The multivocal story uses both Zeke and Ruth's argument about the founding of Tims Creek as well as the voices of the listener (Jimmy Greene), the editor (the fictional Reginald Kain), and, of course, the ultimate author of it all, Randall Kenan, to call attention to the way in which facts gain their essential veracity through repetition and retelling. Much of the interrogation of fact in the final story comes from Kenan's use of the "annotated text," an academic discipline that purports to make provable claims through research and secondary sources. In an interview with Hunt, Kenan said:

> I was tweaking the nose . . . well, I might get in a lot of trouble if I say that. I was playing with academic history as opposed to oral history . . . as opposed to personal history, and memory, and plain old gossip. And how at once they are all very different and disparate, and all very much alike. How often do we look back at something that was written in stone, and not only that, but other people have written about it, you know, and secondary sources have become very influential, and then we see that this former person made all these mistakes. That's an extreme case, and what I was doing was extreme. But looking back on it, it's all sort of subjective, the way we view history. The idea of historiography points out that there are limitations. You may be able to approximate the facts, but there is only one real event, and even that some people would question. To return to physics, theoretically you can't attain the speed of light. Reality in some ways is like that. We can do all sorts of things to approach it, but we can never actually attain it.[8]

Understanding Kenan's use of the annotations to parody how research manufactures its authority reminds us of the flimsy way in which his speakers manufacture their authority—simply through repetition. Zeke begins his narrative of the founding of Tims Creek by saying, "Well, they tell me" (283), and he ends with "All I know is what my granddaddy told me, and boy, that was like I told you" (334).

In a hierarchy of authenticity, a reader is more likely to believe in the kind of claims that have annotations and sources to back them up. Oral narratives lack a cross-referential veracity and often invite skepticism simply because of the form's limitations. In an interview with Malone, Kenan admits, "The speaker has to compress things sometimes, where the writer has the luxury of filling in space, filling in the blanks. There are many more opportunities to deepen and widen a story on the page that the oral storyteller doesn't have. Essentially, writing is largely illusion. Speaking is performance."[9] However, Kenan exposes the authority of academic writing as just as illusory: researchers rely on other academics to substantiate their claims; their writing sits on a scaffolding of repeated and published claims that work to substantiate themselves with each repetition. If academic writing looks down on oral storytelling and its manufacturing of truth through fantasy narratives, Kenan asks his reader to engage with a similar manufactured authority in academic discourse. First, the editor of the text, Reginald Kain, does not exist in physical body; he is a manifestation of the author's academic mind. And yet, his annotations are both real and imaginary. The books he mentions actually exist, or are fabrications, or are mutant hybrids of both research and fiction. The annotations interrupt Zeke's narrative just as Ruth does by pointing out the inconsistencies of the man's story. "There is no documentation of a town or community named Tearshirt in any state or federal files or records," Kain notes (304). That annotation does the same kind of rhetorical work as Ruth's interruption "Don't nobody believe this lie, old man" (329). The only difference between the contestation of fact is that Ruth speaks against Zeke from an alternate oral history, while the fictional Reginald Kain appeals to historical claims.

Kenan's interrogation of history's manufactured authority becomes the focus point of the final story. What we take to be a factual account of actual events boils down to nothing more than a contested narrative with competing alternate stories. As Canon claims, "The intertextuality *Let the Dead Bury Their Dead* maintains within itself results specifically from the title story's subject of Tims Creek's conflicted founding. We see the community as conflicted only through the discrepancies in the oral storytellers and historical documents that pervade the story."[10] History, then, in "Let the Dead Bury Their Dead" amounts to little more than "lies above suspicion," one of Kenan's epigrams from Zora Neale Hurston. It's significant that Kenan uses Hurston to frame his story since, as Harris points out, she was one of the first African American writers to offer the space of the porch as a mediating structure through which competing narratives are given the weight of truth. Critical parts of Kenan's stories take place on the porch. It is on the porch that Maggie realizes that she must follow Reverend Hezekiah out to confront Morton about plowing the field, the final test of her liberation from her old way of thinking. It is on the porch that Stokes confesses to Chi his greatest wish and that, Kenan suggests, the wish is granted. And it is on the porch that Thad reaches out his hand in his one true desire to have some meaningful contact with Essie. The porch is where fantasy becomes truth, imagination becomes memory, and identity becomes communal. It is a site of community, of reaching out, of sharing, and of deciding what the borders are between belief and reality.

However, while the power of the porch does the crucial and uplifting work of community formation, porch talk can also obscure, misrepresent, and disenfranchise those communities it defines as valueless. Cannon claims about *LTDBTD,* "African Americans privilege storytelling as a creator of community, we should not overlook the instability of this activity and its ability to create falsehoods. These falsehoods can and often do become the reality for the African American community at large, and therefore they become standards by which to measure individual realities."[11] It is not an overgeneralization to say that every character in Kenan's collection struggles with what Maggie terms the difference between "What was supposed to be and what truly was" (66). Because the powerful narrative from the town creates its own authority, the force of the manufactured reality works to remove those in the town from the authorship of their own identities. Narratives masquerading as irreproachable belief structures result in most of the tragedies of the book. Clarence Pickett cannot speak to the dead because belief in his gift does not connect with the fundamental Christian belief structures of his family or the town. Essie's scoffing at Thad's homework on evolution forecloses the potential for them to have a meaningful connection and causes the boy to draw up inside himself. And the constant prodding at Mabel Pearsall to be a good wife and mother despite her inward pain causes the woman to create alternate narratives for herself, spaces where she has authority and control. All these situations ultimately become tragic.

And yet, Kenan does suggest that the hybrid world of fact-fiction, of truth-lies, of imaginative-reality is a site that offers the potential for play, expression, and an articulation of some inner truths. His story "This Far" takes the historical figure of Booker T. Washington and imagines him traveling to Kenan's fictional world of Tims Creek. In the story, Washington is a figure to be wondered at; we are not given access to his mind or thoughts except through the lens of our narrator, who speaks to him in the second person. In the story, Washington is a tired man living "someone else's history" (141), and Kenan's imagined fantasy becomes a way for the author to investigate alternative ways of understanding the fraught man's space in African American history. Instead of being a proud soldier of vocational learning, Washington in "This Far" is an unsure and faltering man, capable of being surprised and challenged, feeling hurt and terrified. In the end, Kenan knows that the manufactured intimacy he creates between a real historical figure and an invented narrative within an invented setting is illusory. But, the author celebrates the potential for illusion to open Washington for his readers, to embrace that figure in a way that he could not before. Fantasy opens a door for reclamation, invites transformation and intimacy inside; by the end of the story, Kenan can come to a satisfying conclusion and let Washington's figure go. It is a kind of exorcism in which Washington can stop haunting the author and rest: "So be still, your heart, as you blow out your candle" (162).

### Speaking for/Speaking to the Dead: Interpretations and Queer Knowledges

One of the belief structures the town of Tims Creek uses to enforce its authority is an absolute policing of same-sex intimacy. The gay characters that live in the boundaries of the town can operate only under certain circumstances and inherit strict limits on their freedom and on their expressions of their sexual identity. Dean Williams knows that he has no value in the world of Percy Terrell other than as a kind of disposable vessel for sexual fulfillment. Getting into Percy's truck, Dean considers first that the man is going "to make a sexual proposition. It wouldn't have been the first time a grey-haired granddaddy had stopped his truck and invited Dean in" (165). After all, Dean's sole value in Tims Creek is his appearance—"What did he have to lose? What else did he have to trade on but his looks? A man once told him: Boy, you got eyes that could give a bull a hard-on. Why not use them" (170). And yet, crucially, Dean has no value beyond his looks. He is not allowed an opportunity to speak for himself or to narrate his own value. He is constantly being read, told what he means to his family, to his community. The only person who offers him the ability to narrate his own life is Raymond, the man he is hired to blackmail. Once he learns that Dean tricked him, however, Raymond rejects the young man.

"Don't nobody give a shit about me," Dean tells Raymond at the bar, and his vulnerability about his identity proves to be the thing that makes Raymond fall in love with him. Through Raymond, Dean can finally speak for himself, but when he loses the man who is his link to his value, Dean flounders. Confronting Percy about their deal, Dean threatens to expose their secret to the town. Percy sneers back, "Tell? Who, pray tell, will you tell? . . . And who the *fuck* would believe you?" (187). Terrell's response is almost the same as what Joe Johnson, the truck driver, tells Dean about keeping their relationship a secret: "if you dare tell a soul, it'll be your word against mine, boy And well . . . you'd just be fucking yourself up then" (165). Dean has no voice in Tims Creek. At the heart of *Let the Dead Bury Their Dead,* Kenan poses the question "Who speaks for whom?" What are the consequences of speaking for someone? How do they connect with the ability to speak *to* someone? What knowledge can we glean from hearing the secrets of our family, our community, our town, our region, our church, and why have those secrets been buried for so long? What kind of power do we gain from this queer knowledge?

It is the queer knowledge of Clarence Pickett that frightens the town, though it is not his ability to speak to the dead that scares Tims Creek but rather his ability to speak *for* them. What Clarence represents is the threat to the structure of the town when those who have been wronged and buried can be dug up again. Cannon remarks, "As a gay writer, [Kenan] adds . . . a unique focus on gender and sexuality, which challenges specifically the long-standing institutions of the family and the church in this predominantly African American community. Kenan recognizes that communal beliefs and traditions can prove compromising for those who support them; quite often, the African American community can leave its members tragically mangled and marginalized when they have chosen to participate in less than normative activities."[12] As a symbol of "less than normative activities," Clarence Pickett and his powers threaten Tims Creek. Denying the boy's power does no good, however; because "the evidence kept accumulating and accumulating til you'd have to be deaf, dumb, blind, and stupid to whistle, nod your head, and turn away. But that's exactly what most of us did anyhow. Ain't it strange how people behave?" (14). The town of Tims Creek treats Clarence Pickett the same way it treats Dean Williams—as a potentially threatening figure who will destabilize important belief structures. They ignore both the boy and the man until it is impossible not to—for Dean that means a beating by the Terrell boys and a reminder of his worthlessness, and for Clarence it means a lynch mob chasing Ellsworth Batts to his death.

In "Tell Me, Tell Me," Kenan masterfully connects his meditation on queer knowledge and the consequences of speaking for/to the dead. Throughout the story, Ida Perry is haunted by the spirit of the boy her husband murdered in 1937. The boy stumbled upon Ida and Butch in the middle of a sexual encounter that bordered on bestial—"Butch takes her into the tall grass and takes off her blouse; Butch bites her nipples, hard, and she almost cries" (266). During one of the most intimate moments of her life, a black child appeared; Ida noticed him first and screamed. "A nigger? a little pickaninny? Get out!" Suddenly, the scene became chaotic; Butch's animalistic sexual passion intensified even as he confronted the child. Kicking and hitting the boy, Ida uses the same language as the scene of their sexual liaison: "Butch down on his knees: Butch pushing the boy's face into the sand: Butch's face a wild boar's: punching: kicking: I'll fix you" (267). The man picked up the limp boy and threw him deep into the ocean; he turned triumphantly and smiled at Ida, who manufactured a smile back at her soon-to-be-husband. When Ida chided Butch for his brutish ways, he merely shrugged back: "Just a nigger: Just a nigger" (268). Like Dean Williams, the boy has no voice, no value, no ability to speak for himself. He is marginalized out of the social order of the town and quite literally pushed to the margins of Ida's memory.

In the final moments of "Tell Me, Tell Me," Kenan asks his reader about these "locked away" images: "Why should these memories be disturbed?" What do we gain from this queer knowledge of forgotten suffering, voiceless victims, and invisible pains? Kenan's answer seems to lie in the very ethos of his collection. In speaking for/to the dead, we give a voice to those forgotten, not to seek justice or to right wrongs. The dead do not burst forth from their graves to take vengeance on the living, as Zeke suggests in his history of Tims Creek. Rather, it is the living who must engage with the dead, to offer them their voices as recompense for the ones they were denied while they lived, and open a space for the others who live to walk through and embrace the imagined world of intimacy. That is the true community Kenan imagines in *Let the Dead Bury Their Dead*. "Some things you forget to remain innocent," the author offers as an explanation for Ida's refusal to engage with the ghost of the boy Butch murdered. "Some things you forget to remain free; some things you forget due to lassitude. Moral lassitude, intellectual lassitude, human lassitude" (268). But, in the end, giving one's self permission to forget is an excuse to engage in the thoughtless act of belief without intellectual rigor. The dead demand we hear their voices, and when we do, Kenan suggests through this collection, we hear ourselves, our own shortcomings, our losses, our successes, our victories and violences; in short, we hear our history. That it echoes back to us full of queer secrets should come as no surprise: the dead speak with strange tongues.

# CHAPTER 4

## Brother Baldwin and the Shadow of Tims Creek

> "What I hate about writing non-fiction is that I can't tell the truth. Well, of course, you can tell the truth, but you have to find another way to tell it. I mean, if somebody is sitting there and she reminds you of a bullfrog, in fiction you can say: She put him in mind of a bullfrog. But if you know the woman, the woman is living, and you know the woman is going to read it, you can't say that. That's one of the problems with non-fiction for me. I can't be honest on the same level."
>
> Kenan in conversation with V. Hunt

Randall Kenan's tremendous success as a fiction writer sometimes obscures his accomplishments in other genres—most notably nonfiction, book reviews, criticism, journalism, and personal essays. This chapter chronologically works through Kenan's nonfiction writings and pays special attention to his book-length works. Although the writer has yet to publish a novel or fiction collection since the publication of *Let the Dead Bury Their Dead* in 1992, he has continued to work on a novel that he hopes to publish within the next few years, tentatively titled *There's a Man Going 'Round Picking Names.*

### "Sorrow's Child" (1992)

Kenan's review of Dorothy Allison's debut novel *Bastard Out of Carolina*—released the same year as Kenan's own *Let the Dead Bury Their Dead*—is unique in that the young author seems to be talking to himself about the subject of much of his fiction—the emotional and economic landscape of poor southerners.[1] Calling Allison's novel both "worrisome and brave" (815), Kenan further explains: "Brave because in so many ways this far more bitter than sweet *Bildungsroman*'s real subject is not "Trash" (the name of Allison's prize-winning collection of stories) but the explosive and often difficult to understand world of child abuse; it is also a Faulknerianly bold attempt to plumb the depths of one girl's emotional acceptance, initially, of such cruelty. Yet so closely linked to this story is a particular environment that engenders this particular tragedy that when this environment fails to convince thoroughly, Allison's overarching theme comes dangerously close to running aground. Luckily, she pilots her ship if not always masterfully, often with fine skill" (815).

Kenan is especially anxious over Allison's portrayal of poverty and white trash, which he notes can be tricky to explore without falling into images of "liquored-up, malevolent, unemployed, undereducated, country-music-listening, oversexed, foul-tempered men; and long-suffering, quickly aging, overly fertile, too-young-marrying, hardheaded women" (815). Kenan is especially interested in "the way death functions in the novel—very like the way it functions in Southern life" (816), and a careful reader might find in his obsession with southern death a connection to the author's own exploration of the subject in his fiction. Kenan's conclusion is that Allison has made something true out of her own obsessions—with stereotypes of poverty and trash: "pecan pie and gospel music, snuff-dipping grannies and kissing cousins notwithstanding—*Bastard Out of Carolina* is a singular and important act of art and courage" (816).

### *James Baldwin* (1994)

Kenan's biography of the writer James Baldwin is aimed primarily at young students.[2] Part of Martin Duberman's series *Lives of Notable Gay Men and Lesbians,* Kenan's short biography captures the essential facts about Baldwin's life and work. Kenan's prose in this biography is heavily narrative driven; he offers Baldwin's life as a story with an immediacy that connects young readers to the truth of what it meant to grow up as James Baldwin did, under the tyranny of a brutal father and initiated into the harshness of life as a queer intellectual of color in a country anxious about his very existence. Though the biography uses an economy of language and the immediacy of narrative to connect with its audience, Kenan's focus is laser-tight. One may locate resonances between both writers in Kenan's narration of James Baldwin's life story. It is clear by the end of the biography that Kenan is working through much of his own relationship with the famous author as well as trying to articulate the important moments of Baldwin's life.

### *A Time Not Here: The Mississippi Delta* (1997)

Kenan's essay "That Eternal Burning" shows up late in the progression of photographs that inhabit Norman Mauskopf's collection *A Time Not Here.*[3]

The images that precede Kenan's piece are alternately stark and lush: in black and white, their simple and unadorned aesthetic hearkens back to the work of Walker Evans. Of course, Kenan's poetic essay might then remind a reader of Agee's self-tortured prose in *Let Us Now Praise Famous Men,* a work that also set out to explore the mystery of a region—rural Alabama—through the tools of image and text.

But Kenan's essay works in ways that Agee's does not. He is not interested in telling a single story of the families and men and women and children that Mauskopf presents in his book; instead, Kenan uses his prose to function like the photographs that precede it. He starts by working through Mauskopf's opening image of a boy framed in front of a fire raging before him. As he re-conjures the image in prose, Kenan tries to imagine what that boy might see —"Does he see history, atrocious and bloody? Hear the cries of his mother's giving birth, the muffled clops of mules in the field, the screams of his father being lynched?" The virtual unknowableness of the boy ("He, no more than 13? 12? 11? He with his head full of hip-hop and basketball and comic books and mischief") causes Kenan anxiety but also brings peace. He knows he cannot do anything practical for the boy, but, at the same time, he can try to offer a vessel through which his readers might experience the truths of his existence.

Those truths come to Kenan in the form of Mauskopf's images of the Mississippi Delta, but the author articulates their meaning in a way that photography cannot:

> Land of sorrow, land of sweat, land of memory, land of midnight trains, land of the screech owl and the bear and the katydid and the coon and the timber rattler and the panther, land of tractors, land of foreclosures, land of once-slave and now-freedom, land of money, land of hogs and cows and chickens and turkeys and farm cats and dogs, land of corn and soybean, land of cotton, land of fear, land of hate, land of painful memories, land of God, land of Satan, land of pine and sycamore and spruce and maple and magnolia, land of love, land of heartbreak, land of misery, land of hope. . . . Land of grace. Yet, grace.

In his exploration of the meaning hidden in the photographs, Kenan reimagines their narrative of a continuous story of pain, loss, redemption, and hope. "See history in cotton," he directs his readers: "Cotton can tell a tale." Moving from cotton fields to juke joints to family homes, Kenan imagines the lives of those who haunt Mauskopf's photographs of African Americans in the Delta.

Though there is no direct narrative with a discernible plot, Kenan does move through different settings by jumping in and out of characters' lives;

scarcely do we know who we're inhabiting before Kenan is on to another person and his or her perspective. Perhaps addressing the immediacy of the photographs we have just encountered, Kenan reminds us that these people we view anonymously all have a story: "Each with a face," he reminds us, "though they don't know it, don't realize it—quite unique, touching, if you look, open, full in time transfixed and fixed." "Look," Kenan instructs us, moving from one image, one setting, to the next, always careful to articulate some truth before moving on to the next image. Finally, he settles back to the land itself—"Does the land imagine? Does the land dream," he wonders. Ending with the image of the boy watching the fire, Kenan concludes his essay with the same lack of certainty he found in his opening. "We cannot tell, we cannot know, we do not know, we will not know," he declaims. "This image—just as the cotton fields, the baptism, the hallelujah prayer meetings and the pool hall and the juke joint, yes, even the mothers, the grandmothers . . . are all unknowable . . . this brief burning that lives in the soul of us all."

**"Now Why Come That Is?"** (1998)

First published in Volume 21, Issue One of the journal *Callaloo*—and later reprinted in 2001 in *Callaloo*'s twenty-fifth-anniversary "The Best of *Callaloo Prose*"—Kenan's story explores Tims Creek resident Percy Terrell (familiar to Kenan's readers from *Let the Dead Bury Their Dead*) and his mysterious encounters with a spectral hog that won't seem to leave him alone.[4]

The story opens with Percy in mid-dream; he and Elvis Presley are at a diner with a blonde on each arm. There is a distant bellowing sound that breaks his reverie, and he awakens to a floor soiled with excrement. He tries to get his wife, Rose, to wake and acknowledge the filth, but she simply goes back to sleep. As he cleans up the mess, Percy remembers the first time he saw the hog while working through tax forms in the general store he owned. Sensing a presence, Percy had looked up and seen an enormous hog staring down at him: "A reddish-brown rusty razorback, to be exact, and incisors long enough to be called tusks, kite-big, floppy size of a catcher's mitt" (511). After chasing the beast out of the office and into the store, Percy is no longer able to locate the animal, even though the doors and windows are all locked.

After that first encounter, Percy goes through the motions of his humdrum existence, but nothing feels special or important. He has fantasies of going to Africa and doing big-game hunting, but he finds he is slowly losing his desire to chase and kill animals. Right about the time he forgets about the hog, it makes an appearance again—first at the poultry plant and later in the back of his truck. Each time the hog appears out of nowhere, it disappears just as quickly and mysteriously. Usually no one is there to witness the hog's presence, until the day Percy drives to his son's home for a visit. His grandchildren all come out and notice the hog in the back of the truck; they play with the beast—even going so far as riding him—until Percy shoos the animal away.

Out of options and feeling downright crazy, Percy goes to visit Tabitha McElwaine (also familiar to Kenan's readers) who "all the colored folks [who worked for Percy] swore up and down about . . . who was known throughout five counties as the best mid-wife and rootworker around. They mentioned her name with reverence and a touch of awe" (517). Percy doesn't put a whole lot of faith in Tabitha's powers, and in fact, "when they spoke to him of her, he called them damn fools to their faces, saying they'd be better off just burning their money." Even so, he goes to visit her in her large mansion in town. When he arrives, the hog miraculously appears by his side. Though Tabitha can see the animal, she refuses to help Percy; she claims that he would not be able to do what is required to rid himself of the hog's presence. Furious, Percy leaves.

Arriving home in a tantrum, Percy turns on Hank Williams, pours himself some whiskey, and watches *The Outlaw Josey Wales* on the VCR. He gets drunk for the first time in ages and suddenly has a vision of his old man: "somewhere behind the black label, enlivened by the light of the TV screen, he saw his father, that old demon, with his big black hat with the huge brim, looking down upon his son with contempt. And Percy didn't want to see his father, never ever again, knew he was better than his father, could never be like his father, was a human being person, unlike his father, an evil, freak of nature, yes, he built it all up from nothing, yes, he started it, murdered for it, stole and beat for it, that sonofabitch, and left Percy with the blood" (520).

Drunk and singing Hank Williams at the top of his lungs, Percy turns to see the hog sitting on the couch next to him; he passes out from drunkenness. When he awakens with a hangover, Percy puts himself back together and goes to church. There, at St. Thomas Aquinas Presbyterian Church, close to the end of the preacher's sermon, the hog suddenly bursts into the chapel. Though he is heartened that the congregation at least sees the animal, Percy is horrified that the beast refuses to leave him alone. After toppling him over in front of everyone, the hog makes a break for Percy's house.

Percy pursues the animal and grabs a rifle to shoot it. However, standing with the hog in his sights, Percy finds he cannot shoot him: "They both stood there, stock-still for a period of time Percy could not easily name. Percy and the hog. The hog and Percy. The hog did not move, and by and by, Percy thought: What a magnificent creature. Unaccountably, he began to tremble, and inadvertently, he peered into the hog's eyes, into the depth of them, perhaps toward the soul of it; and to Percy it seemed the hog did the same to him. Percy's trembling increased, and a feeling began to wash over him and into him, and Percy began to feel puny. Naked. Ashamed . . . that all he had he and his father had stolen and robbed for, and that he had no right to any of it" (522).

Unable to shoot the hog, Percy breaks down into sobs and tears. The gun slips from his hands, and the hog leaps in the air at the man. Covering his face for the impact, the next sound he hears is his wife's voice checking to see if he is all right. But Percy is too far into his lonesome sobbing to answer her.

There are many elements to "Now Why Come That Is" that connect with Kenan's other works. First and foremost, the story focuses on a kind of haunting, a visitation, though, unlike the demons of Kenan's first novel, the ghost that seems to follow Percy around comes in the form of an animal. We are unsure just why such a spirit takes the form of a hog, but then, the answer might be simply that Percy is being tormented by something primal, bestial, powerful, with a splendor that is reserved for the untamed. So much of Kenan's description of the hog focuses on its visceral power, often centered in its prodigious genitals. And when Percy has his final confrontation with the spirit at the end, he recognizes his feeling of hopelessness as a similar feeling to "when he discovered that his penis was not the largest in creation and that the juice of his testicles would neither save nor solve humanity; neither save nor solve himself" (522).

Only once Percy senses his ultimate powerlessness in the face of the beast is he finally free of its torment. In a way, then, the structure of the story follows the "Christmas Carol" plot progression of *Visitation*. Percy, as the Scrooge stand-in, is quite literally visited by fantastical spirits (we can count the hog, Tabitha, and the conjured image of his father as his three kinds of ghosts) and is forced to come to terms with his limitations and selfishness before experiencing a dark night of the soul. Once confronted with the truth of his identity, Percy releases his control to the beast and breaks down into a tottering childish weeping. He has come through, has been transformed by, his experience with the animal, and perhaps has taken the first step toward a personal transformation.

Kenan also comes back to the word "queer" often in the story: Percy casts a "queer spell" (515) over the meeting when he prattles on about the hog; the hog's presence is a "queer reality" (516) that Percy must learn to get used to in his day-to-day life. The repetition of "queer" throughout the story reminds us again of the potent sexuality of the beast haunting Percy and of the possibility for epiphanies through the strangest of mediums. For Kenan, queerness is a vehicle that allows his characters to encounter the truest version of themselves. And finally, queerness marks the divisions of power that exist within Tims Creek, divisions that run on both racial and economic lines. Percy feels grievously disconnected from the "uppity coloreds" (515) and the "colored folks who worked for him" (517). He also must work through divisions in himself—trying to locate the gaps between who his father was and what he became, for example—but he is crucially unable to connect the gaps between those over whom he has power and his identity as their employer, a fellow citizen. It is this queer inability to imagine the lives of others that seems to prompt the emergence of the hog and the message of his crucial impotence—despite his economic and cultural potency—that the specter seems to evoke in the old man's consciousness.

### *Walking on Water: Black American Lives at the Turn of the Twenty-First Century* (1999)

> "When people think about African Americans, they think about the urban North and the rural South. I mean, there are anomalies like Los Angeles, but most think of that as something of an extension of New York—the only difference being that the sun shines there and it's warm all the time.[5] But that's the way the American imagination deals with black folk. What I'm saying is: Look, there are black folk in New England, Martha's Vineyard, and Vermont. There are black folk in Nova Scotia, and they have been there as long as there have been black people on this continent. There are black people in Montreal who speak French. There are black people all over: Alaska, the Great Basin, everywhere. How does that affect the way we look at black people overall? A lot of the things that we are saying that might be true for blacks in the rural South and blacks in the North may not be true for people in these other regions. And if not, what does that mean about all of us?"[6]

Kenan's 1999 book, *Walking on Water,* part of a two-book deal negotiated with Knopf that also included *Let the Dead Bury Their Dead,* has an elegantly simple premise: Kenan decides that, to understand what it means to be black in America, he will travel all over the country, talk to various constituencies of black Americans (of all classes and regions), and work through their stories to form some conclusion. What follows in the 670-plus-page volume is a litany of narratives and stories that Kenan collects that inevitably complicate, rather than illuminate, both his aim and the mystery of American blackness. In his introduction, Kenan admits that "before I even begin . . . this work—in the end—is a failure" (xi); instead, Kenan sees it as "an arrogant proposal . . . doomed at its inception by the physical and intellectual impossibility of capturing successfully 36 million souls." His introduction-conclusion is that the question he sought to answer—"What does it mean to be black?"—really can't be answered with facts because "this is essentially a spiritual question, involving belief, myth, desire, longing, some history, much faith." In short, the book project transforms Kenan more than he transforms the book, and *Walking on*

*Water* becomes less a volume that situates American blackness in the dawning of a new millennium and more a book about Kenan himself: "a personal response to all the people and places I have met over the years of my travels across North America . . . a subjective response to a subjective question; an existential answer to a query about being." *Walking on Water* is, finally, as Hovis claims, "at its base an aggressively intertextual work [that] makes use of a vast diversity of oral and written sources, including those that promote the healthiness of the very postmodern identity that troubles and entices [Kenan]."[7]

Kenan starts his journey to understand "blackness" in Massachusetts; he is in search of the black "middle class," but he finds almost immediately that he has to be clearer for those he interviews, including Dora Grain, who gained fame in 1983 when she pushed back against the assumption that all African Americans on Martha's Vineyard had to live in one specific region, Oak Bluffs. When Kenan asks her about the representation of the black middle class, she pushes back: "You mean somebody who is financially well off?" (22). With Grain as his first subject, Kenan tries to untangle the myth of class, region, and place with an authentic version of American blackness. "What I resent," Grain tells him, "is the idea that 'In New York, all blacks live in Harlem.' . . . That to me is a racist assumption. All blacks on Martha's Vineyard do not live in Oak Bluffs . . . it's a racist attitude." It's important, then, that in Kenan's first section, one he titles "In Thoreau's Backyard," he goes in search of American blackness in a region where it might seem least visible, New England. The locales of Martha's Vineyard; Burlington, Vermont; and Bangor, Maine, do not immediately strike a reader as sites of African American authenticity. And yet, the people he meets there identify, to varying degrees, with their conception of blackness. One such woman, Paige Wadley-Bailey, of Burlington, reminds Kenan of "those women who surrounded me in my youth, like Miss Nellie Mae and Miss Clem—strong church women who could do almost anything, you suspected" (73).

Even so, early on in his trip through New England, Kenan finds himself having a difficult time reconciling his subjects' views with his own: "I had set out to figure out for myself what it meant to be black. The few people with whom I had spoken did share some of my obvious notions, and yet they were also at times wildly at odds with my own, and with each other. What the hell was I trying to accomplish?" (76). The complicated entangling of his subjects' thoughts on race—as well as the critical connections with (and disconnections from) Kenan's own view on his blackness—pick up a frenzy that haunts the remainder of the book. And the central guiding question of the book shifts early on from "What is American blackness?" to "What the hell am I trying to accomplish?" Kenan finds that, far from what he had imagined, the African Americans he encounters in places like Bangor and Burlington don't feel displaced from a larger conception of authentic blackness. "Oh, I might have missed a lot of good parties," one Maine resident tells him, but "our culture was just the same culture as anyplace else" (85).

Breaking west from New England, Kenan travels across what he calls "The Great Big Middle," and his journey makes up the second section of *Walking on Water.* He travels to places like Buffalo, New York; Madison, Wisconsin; and Coeur d'Alene, Idaho, as well as to more prominent spaces of black imagination such as Chicago, Illinois. In these places, the people who Kenan encounters more compellingly connect with the author's conception of blackness. One person tells him, "Being black . . . I'll tell you, if you don't start out being aware of it, experience will remind you" (114). In Chicago, Kenan turns inward, and, instead of interviewing a wide variety of residents, he explores his own conception of the city in a section called "My Own Private Chicago": "Black life in Chicago, the black history of Chicago, is immense and impressive . . . makes one wonder why Harlem has received so much more ink. A rich past so vast and deep that I felt crushed by it. I felt crushed, particularly, by the weight and significance of what colored so much black life in Chicago, namely the mass influx of black folk from the first decade of the twentieth century until late in the 1960s . . . perhaps I am prejudiced; perhaps I am too influenced by the old views of Upton Sinclair and stories of Richard Daley . . . perhaps I was not ready to shed my own tainted vision of the place, to rework the details and come up with a fresh notion; perhaps it can't be done. Perhaps I failed" (155).

Kenan's imagination is much more agile with regard to places like St. Paul, Minnesota, or Coeur D'Alene, Idaho, spaces whose history of blackness and populations are far less gargantuan and unwieldy. There, he finds his voice and understands his evolving task a little bit better. Ending his section on St. Paul/Minneapolis, Kenan assures himself, "I felt, for the first time in a long time, that I was beginning to ask the right questions" (200).

In his brief third section, Kenan visits lands of "The Ice Mystique"—Maidstone, Saskatchewan, and Anchorage, Alaska. Maidstone provides Kenan with a bit of a letdown. He asks a local librarian for "black people" and receives the sorry reply, "I'm so, so sorry, but all our *Newgrews* moved away years ago" (254). Even so, Kenan locates a tight-knit community and is taken in by the locals. "Nothing could have prepared me for British Columbia's ever-changing and magisterial poetry," he writes in the opening section on Anchorage, "Cold Hands and Fiery Hearts." The black population of Anchorage is sparse but powerful. Evelyn Bailey, who runs a beauty parlor in town, reminds Kenan of the struggle to even exist in such a territory: "You've got to know what you got to do to make it up here. . . . The parents that's up here have got to be strong, to raise children up here, and make sure they know how to stay out of trouble" (284).

Section four examines "Our Still Frontier": Seattle, San Francisco, Oakland, Los Angeles, the mythic cities of the American West. Seattle is, to Kenan, "a place defined in the American mind as a City on the Edge of Forever—as the American frontier knocks on the door of our own finitude. . . . We need a place where the frontier continues. And Seattle, wild and tamed, simple and sophisticated, plain and complicated, remains fixed . . . in that constant state of yearning" (302–303). In Seattle, Kenan meets with the novelist Charles Johnson, author of *Middle Passage.* Johnson introduces Kenan to James Washington Jr., "a latter day griot" (304). With Washington and, later, with a new friend, Jeff Henderson, Kenan is introduced to a vision of Seattle that connects deeply with his conception of it as the new frontier. In the black imagination, Seattle works as a space where one can "glare into the future and summon" an image of possibility that might lead to intellectual and emotional freedom, to "make it into something Mississippi could never be" (326).

In "The There There," Kenan travels through San Francisco, into Oakland, and finally down into southern California—to Los Angeles and Allensworth. In the Bay Area, Kenan finds old friends who take him into Oakland and "art galleries full of black and African art, and shops and parks, and a soul food restaurant whose owners I met, folk from Texas . . . a mall thronged with black teenagers . . . suddenly I was in a true hub of black America again" (328). And yet, after all his journeys north and through the sparse populations of African Americans, this nexus of cultural activity presents itself as a strange familiarity—"Did I look at it differently?" he asks himself. "Remembering Chicago," he explains to his readers, "I quickly decided to forgo attempting to plumb the depths of the Bay Area—too large, too confusing, too new in too many ways" (336). Kenan explores the figure of Mary Ellen Pleasants, a civil rights activist whose history in the area is often celebrated as a marker of the region's diversity.

Driving south, Kenan turns witty: "I have seen the future, and it is not Los Angeles," he tells his readers. "Los Angeles looks exactly like what it is: an anomaly built on the desert, a futuristic nexus, a meeting place of far-flung cultures" (341). When he visits with Dr. Rick Moss, Kenan gets an education about California's importance in the struggle for freedom. "If you look at any publication on civil rights, you'll see Alabama and Mississippi and Georgia, but you won't see California. . . . You know there are folks here doing it. They weren't slaves. They were free black people and they were industrious. They were educated, trained. . . . And so, that's an important part of our history" (345). Kenan finds in his conclusion of the fourth section that his exploration of the West has proved something of a mixed bag: "California is the most populous state in the union.. . . . The idea that I could address even a fraction of what it meant to be black in that state made me weak at the knees. To be sure, California proved my original point: it contained every possible element of African American diversity—descendants of pioneers, displaced southerners, Africans, West Indians, people of every possible mixture and hue; it had a north and a south and a middle; it had rich and poor and working classes. California was quintessentially American, yet somehow America distorted, somehow warped, somehow refracted" (349).

But what is compelling to Kenan about California is how it sustains itself in that warped and warping vision of American identity; even if all that is left is "remnants of a dream" (Hollywood, the ocean, economic mobility), "yet . . . [the] dream lived on. *We are such stuff as dreams are made on*. . . . Once upon a dream. . . . " (392).

The fifth section—"Promised Lands"—starts with an exploration of Las Vegas, which Kenan labels "The American City." Moving into chapter 16 and the last three sections of the book, the reader understands the strengths of Kenan's book: he has a keen eye for place and setting, and one of the book's success is its work as a kind of travelogue. *Walking on Water* finds its voice, even as the nominal focus on American blackness gets muddied. "Only in Las Vegas did I realize that I was truly American," Kenan claims, "for in Las Vegas, the sin, the tawdriness, the sheer tackiness, and the vanity and the frailty and the banality, and yes, the humanity, of our country is front and center, so neon bright and unapologetic, that the only honest response can be love" (395). Kenan marries his unease with the city to the dissonances that arise in the claiming of American identity in general and, by acknowledging their connection, finds a means through which to celebrate Las Vegas. He meets with Edith Jackson, a local tutor who works with the Clark County literacy program; Jackson instructs Kenan on how, in the middle of this very American city of opportunity and promise, there are no resources or opportunities for its black residents: "Blacks in this town do not have a voice in anything that has to do with government" (400), she confides to Kenan. In the next chapter of the fifth section, Kenan strikes out for Salt Lake City, and, instead of mediating the words of the people he meets, he presents them in bare transcription; for example he quotes Nathan Gray, who says, "It was worse down South—but up here, you wasn't used to it, like you was down South" (447).

In the final two chapters of section five, Kenan explores Cheyenne, Wyoming, and Denver, Colorado, part of the mythic "West" that enchanted him as a young boy. "Of all the frontier towns, Dodge City, Silver City, Tombstone, none conjures up the romance quite like ole Cheyenne," he claims (451). And yet, in Cheyenne, Kenan locates some of that youthful exuberance in the family of Senator Harriet Elizabeth Byrd. It's a feeling he cannot conjure in the bleak dirt of Denver, a city awash in "the blend of that very past with [the city's] outsized dreams of Manifest Destiny mingled with a new rugged and demanding yuppism and the postindustrialization of the future" (474). In Denver, Kenan attends a "black rodeo" (486) and finds the surreal scene a prodding question for black Americans: "What is Manifest Destiny? What is Destiny? What or who makes it Manifest? Will the truth make us free?" (491). Kenan doesn't get to a solid answer by the end of the fifth section, but he comes to the beginning of something that feels like a conclusion: "I was beginning to believe . . . that destiny had something greater in store for the descendants of the slaves. But this was just a feeling, unscientific and personal—just a feeling" (500).

By the time readers reach the sixth section of *Walking on Water,* they find themselves coming south again and into regions and spaces more commonly associated with black communities and culture, such as Lafayette, Louisiana, the subject of Kenan's twentieth chapter. With the guidance of insurance officer Don Cravin, Kenan tries to piece together the nomenclature of Louisiana and how it informs the state's people and its politics. The word "creole" especially fascinates Kenan, who calls upon Ruth Foote, the editor of the *Creole* magazine, to help him understand all the connotations of the contested word. Foote tells Kenan, "'Creole' means a lot of different things. There's a million different definitions for it. . . . What we're used to, our food, our music. . . . Because a Creole can mean a pitch-black person or a light-skinned person. . . . It can mean somebody from Haiti. Or New Orleans Creole" (517–518). Kenan also tries to understand the origins and mystique of zydeco: he learns that "zydeco is the Creole word for snap beans. . . . Nowadays, Zydeco should be quickly recognized by the brassy, fluty sound of the accordion, and the gritty, scratching *frottoir* or a washboard or rub board" (528). After spending time in the company of zydeco musicians and among the vibrant cultures and music of Lafayette, Kenan leaves the city regretfully: "I felt as if I were leaving home," he says (540).

The final chapter of section six gives Kenan the title for his entire project: "Walking on Water." The chapter starts with Kenan in Atlanta, Georgia, where he is promoting the 1992 collection *Let the Dead Bury Their Dead*. As he is held in an elevator at the CNN Center while a "'mob' of teenagers" riots outside, Kenan flashes forward to 1993 and the origins of the Students for Afrikan Amerikan Empowerment (SAAE) movement, which "rose up from the battlegrounds of Atlanta's Rebellion of April 29th and 30th, 1992, after the verdict in the Rodney King case was announced" (545). Kenan finds hope in the students' movement: "After all my traveling, after seeing the good, the bad and the indifferent, I found this movement to have been undeniably one of the most encouraging and exciting developments among African Americans. I thought of Nat Turner, Gabriel Prosser, Denmark Vesey, Cinque, Harriet Tubman—men and women who had no alternative but to fight, to use violence against a system that would listen to no other appeal. I thought of Ida B. Wells, Mary McLeod Bethune, Frederick Douglass, and perhaps most forcefully, Thurgood Marshall—warriors all, irreducibly and irrefutably locked at times in mortal combat with a wicked government . . . the strength of African Americans has always been that their position was (is) a moral one" (557).

After his heartening experience with the SAAE, Kenan turns to St. Simons, a site of exotic beauty that exists almost mythically in Kenan's imagination (thanks, in large part, to its being the setting for the film *Daughters of the Dust*). At Igbo Landing in 1803, a mutiny aboard the slave ship the *York* ended in the deaths of twelve members of the Igbo tribe. It is from this story that Kenan finds the metaphor for his project.

"Matter, physical matter as we know it, exists in four states," Kenan explains, "solid, liquid, gas, plasma." The rules of physical matter relate to the division between molecules: "the reason a human being is unable to walk on water is due to the fact that his molecules, being in a solid state, move more slowly than those molecules in liquid (water)—they are out of molecular sync" (587). Kenan contextualizes that kind of "book" knowledge with the faith that it takes to believe in something—"That is another kind of knowledge," he explains (588). "It is not inconceivable that I am the descendant of one of those survivors of that day back in 1803," he concludes. And, by the end of his chapter, Kenan makes clear that maybe belief is the stronger of the two: "The evidence of things not seen and the substance of things yet to come. . . . This next thing I had to do was to keep this faith, and that was a personal mission" (601).

Kenan's final section brings him back "home," where he finds that his trip has changed him: place and space seem to be transformational in a way that he had not anticipated. The first chapter of the final section takes place not in a concrete setting but in "cyberspace." Kenan works through personal history in this penultimate chapter. To answer the question "What is blackness," he finds he must first answer "Who am I?" Kenan locates the answer to the ever-nagging question of identity in the rooted community of the cyberspace, where identity exists outside of our body: "This thing we call being black, does it exist outside of our bodies" he muses: "Where, indeed, am I black? On my skin? In my mind?" (621).

In the final chapter of *Walking on Water,* Kenan doesn't so much come to a conclusion about the questions that have been dogging him during his travel and writing as he comes to a place of rest. Significantly, he ends his journey not in Chinquapin but in New York, his adopted homeland and his literal birthplace. "And in many ways it was fitting for me to think of New York, and not North Carolina, as home, for, in the most basic of senses, it was my home. It was the place where I was born; it was the place where I had made my living and the bulk of my life for the last eight years" (633). At home in his city, Randall Kenan finally "sees" what he has accomplished with such a huge project: "I realized later that my dream was undoable and yet done, for on my table rested not interviews and notes and thoughts, but a record of my personal history of the last six years. No longer was this about gathering facts—though I had facts aplenty. It was about feeling and interpretation and ways of seeing the world and of being in the world. The truth is there are over thirty-six million ways to be black, from the curious guy who raises pigeons on the roof across the street from me . . . to the Tennessee mountain minister who teaches Greek and Latin . . . to the NBA player from Lake Charles, Louisiana. . . . But to bear witness I need only one soul, and my soul is a witness" (637).

Kenan finds in the articulation of his perspective and in his soul-song a fitting place to rest after his long journey across the country. It is a "strange peace" to know that understanding blackness actually involves self-exploration and acknowledgment of your "contradictions" (639). And, for Kenan, that project ends in a site of familiarity and love.

### *The Fire This Time* (2007)

With a shout-out to Baldwin's seminal 1963 essay collection *The Fire Next Time*,[8] Randall Kenan namechecks his spiritual and literary mentor and offers seven essays that examine the connections among history, racial identity, and legacies. Published in 2007 by Melville House, the collection was, according to Kenan, "the idea of my editor and publisher, Dennis Loy Johnson," who encouraged the author to thread a series of essays together that would pay homage to Baldwin's intellectual legacy and explore Kenan's complicated musings on race and personal history.

The collection opens with a short essay—"The Fire This Time"—that introduces the reader to Baldwin. Kenan offers an immediate personal (and biographical) connection with the writer, who, like Randall Kenan, was "an out of wedlock child" from parents "of the South" (11). He goes on to introduce the intellectual terrain of his collection by explaining the conditions that led to Baldwin's publishing *The Fire Next Time*. Kenan notes that Baldwin's ethos was marked by a "high standard of truth-telling—hard truths, difficult truths, truths about race" (13). Ending the essay with a direct quotation from *Notes of a Native Son*, Kenan sets the tone for the essays that follow: a direct confrontation with "commonplace" injustices and the "charge to keep my own heart free of hatred and despair."

In the next essay, Kenan writes directly to his godson, Jailen; he starts by remembering the boy's grandfather, John Wallace Brown, who "took a shine to me straightaway" (19). Kenan recounts his obsession with Brown, how he "dressed like a duke and carried himself like a crown prince. . . . He was independent, but not haughty. He believed in decency and courtesy" (20). Kenan explains to Jailen how his grandfather joined the "Fire and Rescue Squad," where "few of the black men of the community felt welcome" (20). At the annual pig-pickin', Kenan remembers he would stay up all night with Brown helping to roast the hog. While there, the man was often called to rescue Kenan's classmates, one the victim of a "fatal gunshot wound" (22). Kenan ends his letter to Jailen by explaining how his grandfather, John Wallace Brown, was a spiritual heir of sorts to him: as he traveled the country for his book *Walking on Water,* Kenan would come back to the lessons Brown had taught him: "Of the many things I learned from all the people I've written about across North America . . . the thing that forged who they were . . . was this sense of family" (22). Kenan counsels the boy that many will see him as "a demon . . . the young African American male. *The black male*" (23). But Kenan asks Jailen to think about how he is seen and to reimagine his value as one of freedom: "Did you know once upon a time, black folk could fly," he concludes. "A hidden truth. A metaphor. . . . Remember that when you think you are stuck in the mud" (24). Connecting his letter to Jailen to his next essay, "Sorrow Songs," is an epigraph from the Toni Morrison novel *Song of Solomon:* "If you surrender to the air, you can ride it."

In "Sorrow Songs," Kenan uses the framing device of the story of Crystal and Travis, a mother and son in Memphis, Tennessee, who came to the attention of the nation in 2000 because of Crystal's sudden death from lung cancer. Horrified at the prospect of going into foster care, Travis lived with his dead mother for thirty-three days until a family friend came by to check on them both. Haunted by the real-world tale, Kenan decided to make a story out of it, for stories, he claims, allow "us to slip into another's soul for a short period" (30). But, Kenan notes, the story is almost an inadequate genre for such a tale; he suggests instead that it might be best expressed as what W.E.B. Du Bois terms "a sorrow song." Turning to Du Bois, Kenan examines his life, including his exile in Ghana, and wonders what Du Bois would think of the contemporary state of American racial politics (he mentions the O.J. Simpson trial, the J.F.K. assassination, the 1992 Los Angeles riots that followed the trial of policemen who beat a young Rodney King, and the attacks of September 11). Working through America's thorny history of race, authority, and anxiety around black men (Kenan mentions Clarence Thomas and Hurricane Katrina "looters"), Kenan explains that these incidents are "symptomatic of the current state of race relations in the fifty states . . . fear of the violent black male, dread of miscegenation, poor black folk as victims of their own doings, law enforcement acting like a lynch mob, and underneath it all . . . a decided need to blame somebody" (38–39). In the end, Kenan returns to his framing device—the story of Crystal and Travis; he remarks that he is sure now that such a story needs to be a sorrow song, a blues song: because "the blues heal" (40). "Perhaps if I were a songwriter," he concludes, "I could begin to do honor to that singular story of Travis and his personal horror . . . but . . . I'll just have to trek on in flatfooted prose" (41).

In "Brother Rabbit versus Brother Fox," Kenan begins with his earliest memory—the death of his great uncle: "I remember that particular late September day . . . my uncle said he wasn't feeling well" (46). The boy lies down next to him on a quilt his mama brought out for him to play on, and "by and by one of the ladies came to check on him. He wouldn't wake up" (47). Kenan turns from that morbid memory and his fear of the dark ("Was it death I feared, or simply sleep?" he asks) into a meditation on the "Black Old Guard," a subculture Kenan remembers first encountering in high school when he found a book by Stephen Birmingham titled *Certain People: America's Black Elite.* The teenage Kenan "devoured" the book: "so strange and unusual, and somehow instructive . . . this vision of a high-born, high-living colored aristocracy fascinated my eyes" (50). The objective correlative of Kenan's aristocratic fantasies was John H. Johnson, "the richest black man in America" (51), a figure Kenan at first tried to emulate, but one he later began to indict for materialism.

Weaving his own memories of helping Brown build the family home, Kenan engages with the story of Brer Fox and Brer Rabbit, especially the story of the "briar patch," a place into which Brer Rabbit tricks Brer Fox into throwing him—though the rabbit is immune to the thorns of his ancestral home. Kenan picks apart the symbols Joel Chandler Harris uses in his Uncle Remus tales and relates them to African traditions ("Rabbits are not only lucky, but they are the masters of mother wit," he explains [61]). That spirit of Brer Rabbit exists, Kenan argues, even in contemporary imaginings of black culture, even though statistics of incarceration, drug use, and illiteracy are highest in black communities.

Kenan argues that the spirit of Brer Fox is also "an equal part of Black America" (65). Kenan recounts the story of LBJ's passing of the Civil Rights Act of 1964 as a central moment when the "solid South" became the seat of far-right conservatism. Brer Fox might be alive and well in the conservative south;

Kenan suggests that his duplicitous nature might exist in the mind of Clarence Thomas or Condoleezza Rice. These black conservative figures remind Kenan of Booker T. Washington and his famous Atlanta Exposition Address, when he counseled black workers to "cast down your buckets where you are." These "foxy elite conservatives," as Kenan calls them, routinely use the language of "tough love" to decry social programs meant to help the inner cities (70–71). "The real danger that attends the arrival of Brother Fox in the once binary black-white equation of racial relations," Kenan explains, "is that he muddies the moral power of what was once unassailable" (75). Even so, Kenan ends his essay by arguing that the role of Brother Fox is not a scorched-earth trope: the fox "uses cunning in a different way than Brother Rabbit does" (77).

In his next essay, "An Ahistorical Silliness," Kenan opens with his early desires to write back to the authors he was reading as a boy—Edgar Allan Poe, Beatrix Potter, and Robert Louis Stevenson. Kenan shifts to a memory from his seventh-grade year when his teacher, Miss Underwood, required him to come up with a personal manifesto. Kenan went on to write "a paragraph that essentially looked down its nose at what Flannery O'Connor once called Good Country People" (83). In front of the class, a young Randall Kenan "read it with conviction . . . a heartfelt though misguided declaration of self-help and self-empowerment." When the class and teacher responded with derision, Kenan sought solace from his family, who took turns reading the paragraph in silence. Instead of being comforted, Edythe asked him the terrifying question "Who do you think you are?" (85) and forced him to rewrite the essay. In working through the essay, Kenan learned that his father, Harry, had murdered Miss Underwood's brother.

The essay shifts to Kenan remembering a visit to his father in prison. The young boy gained a kind of schoolyard capital by having a "father who could be viewed as a piratical ne'er do well" and an absent mother, Clara, who barely saw her son when she came for visits. "To say that our relationship was broken would be too presumptuous," Kenan muses of Clara. "It would propose some foundation that was never truly constructed" (87). Turning from his memories of his family, Kenan muses on how America privileges anti-intellectualism; we see race "rooted in the idea of skin color, not culture; it is superstition, not science" (90). Kenan mourns the current state of our discourse on race and its lack of imagination, especially because, "once upon a time, not too very long ago, the debate . . . about race was much more visceral" (94). As an example of this historical moment, Kenan mentions the sport of boxing and how it represented the problems of racial identity throughout the twentieth century with figures like Jack Johnson and Joe Louis. Working through Cassius Clay's reemergence as Muhammad Ali to George Foreman's criminality, Kenan constructs African

American boxing icons as emblematic of the shifting work done on behalf of race in American culture.

As a final meditation, Kenan works through "Negroes' seeming affection for the word 'nigger'" (102). Using Randall Kennedy's history of the word, Kenan offers different cultural and historical connotations for "nigger" in its use by African Americans. Using Richard Pryor's famous decision to stop using the word in his comedy routines, Kenan remarks, "Some would have us believe that the word is so blood-soaked, so scornful, such a thing-maker, that to breath it is to . . . buy into the overarching, all-powerful worldview of White Supremacy" (106). Kenan remains skeptical of the power of the word ("At the end of the day it really is just a word, children," he explains [107]). Kenan ends with his grandfather's blindness from an injury he suffered while working on the house, and his conclusion works into the final line: "it's all about learning how to see" (111).

"There Is a River" begins with Kenan exploring the connection between religion and politics. Kenan notes that "since before Emancipation, the Black Church" has always emphasized "uplift, community, the care and upkeep of the soul, and a loud voice against injustice" (114). However, Kenan notes that the focus of the church has shifted: "Where is the Black Church now?" he asks (115). The tradition of the black church as an instrument for revolution and a resource for civil rights is slowly shifting into an agency for capitalism and self-aggrandizement, Kenan argues. For a good portion of "There Is a River," Kenan works through the history of activism within the black church; he looks at figures such as Vernon Johns and Dr. Martin Luther King Jr.

In his section "The Fruit of Islam," Kenan turns to the historical association between black individuals and the founding of the Nation of Islam, in 1931; he emphasizes that Islam's peaceful connection (the word means "peace," he reminds his readers at the end of that section) is being lost in the wake of September 11, 2001. Amid his ruminations on religion, Kenan also mentions his father's devout adherence to the tenets of Jehovah's Witnesses. He recounts an experience as a teenager when he went with his father to a meeting and encountered all different races and ethnicities interacting as equals: "I had never been around so many white folk who treated me like one of the crowd. It was downright unsettling," he remembers (126). Years later, his father is asked to be an elder, and at a ceremony he cannot attend, Kenan meditates on a snapshot of his father from that event: "How odd that now he is the man of God and I am the sinner, the Christian agnostic apostate" (127). He ends his essay by circling back to the trickster figures of the fox and the rabbit as well as the importance of the "sorrow song" that religion offers African Americans in the form of the protest song.

The final essay of the collection, "Nevermore," brings the series of essays full circle as Kenan ends with the image of black bodies as "ravens," people who "took wing" and learned to fly (134). The figure of the raven, Kenan argues, is a new type of black individual—people who wear "their blackness proudly, like an overcoat against the weather" (134); an example of this type of figure is Oprah Winfrey, whom Kenan defines as "a nonjudgmental sister-critic. . . . She is the older sister who has your back . . . yet who can, with arms akimbo, tell you the painful truth about yourself" (136). As a corollary to the rise of Oprah, Kenan also mentions Barack Hussein Obama, who "represents a new paradigm, both political and social" (137). In fact, Obama becomes a central focus of Kenan's concept of the raven: "Obama flies, without a doubt. But his magic, that voodoo that he do so well is bound up in blackness. Not despite, but because of. A certain romance attends him, an aura, a mystery—is he black or half-African? What does African American mean? What does his stance on race mean to me?"

At the time of the composition of this essay, Obama was just a senator, but Kenan predicts that, should he win the presidency, it will be because of his blackness, not despite it. That he is a raven, however, makes him no less a trickster figure, a trope in African American popular culture that includes such figures as the Wayans brothers or Robin Givhan or Neil DeGrasse Tyson. Kenan mentions these figures "as being emblems of a new Negro. . . . I cannot get over . . . how little is made of their obvious and undeniable blackness" (143).

Even so, Kenan is quick to note that this reading of blackness is available only to a select few, and so the challenge remains to unite two disparate communities under the banner of African American culture: "that of the New Middle Class, a black intelligentsia given new and larger wings by meritocracy, owing much to the successes of the Civil Rights Movement, the very real gains of affirmative action, and their own pluck and luck; and that of the negro vox populi, the masses of black folk, Brother Rabbit still largely an underclass despite the gains of the last hundred and two score years, still underemployed, undereducated, underrepresented . . . still used as pawns by a media and by the political classes who care more about digits than people" (143–144).

Kenan calls that new Negro "Brother Raven. Unpredictable. With aspects of both Brother Fox and Brother Rabbit—usually the best of their attributes" (145). Kenan ends with James Baldwin—he imagines the moment that Baldwin learns of the assassination of Martin Luther King Jr. and how the writer must have been disgusted by the deaths of so many leaders he had come to admire—Medgar Evers, King, Malcolm X. And yet, Kenan's final message to Baldwin through the essay is one of hope; there is a new possibility coming, he seems to suggest in his final lines: "The beauty is still here, Jimmy, and it is more glorious, more dazzling, and infinitely more transforming than any of us could have dreamed . . . a change is gonna come, baby. Hold on. Curse me for a fool, but I think the time is now. I believe I am a witness. I've seen the ravens begin to take wing" (149). Just a year after the publication of his collection, Kenan saw the election of Barack Obama as president of the United States of America.

*The Cross of Redemption: Uncollected Writings* (2010)

In this collection of Baldwin's uncollected essays, articles, reviews, and interviews, Randall Kenan curates a series of writings that have never before been published in book form.[9] Writing in the introduction, Kenan might as well be addressing his twenty-something self in New York City: "In this exciting Manhattan Village," he asks his reader to imagine what it would be like to be James Baldwin as a young man: "you meet a lot of politically noisy, rambunctious, revolutionary, bohemian, fun-loving types, people who follow socialist ideals . . . but you also meet musicians, singers, theater people of all stripes, public intellectuals, writers and editors" (xvi). Kenan concludes the opening of his introduction by explaining that at barely twenty-four, Baldwin had already become an intellectual force, a position in American letters that he would cement years later: "By the time of his first publication James Baldwin was already onto his second, or even third, life" (xvii).

Even as we feel as if we "know" Baldwin, Kenan explains—through his overly personal essays, his recounting of his biography, his gargantuan presence in popular culture and literature—"there yet remains an impenetrable mystery, still surrounding James Baldwin . . . almost like that of a character from the very Dickens novels he loved so much—rising up, phoenix-like, on the wings of a literary archangel" (xix). It is with this mystery in mind that Kenan shares the celebration of exposure to new works to Baldwin's words: "A new glimpse into the probable impossibility that is James Baldwin is a welcome treat and a treasure." The guiding principle of the volume Kenan has edited is to introduce readers to "a GPS map of the geography of [Baldwin's] mind's progress" (xix) by presenting us with "a collection of snapshots. A sketchbook" of the author's intellect at work.

Following a brief chronology of Baldwin's major works, Randall Kenan gets real with his audience about Baldwin's appeal to writers: "he was audacious in his love for complex sentences . . . death-defying sentences. Lush romantic sentences. Sentences that dared to swallow the entire world" (xxii–xxiii). Though he was a novelist primarily, "Baldwin unleashed his most baroque prose in his nonfiction" (xxiii), Kenan asserts: "Reading a Baldwin sentence can feel like recreating thought itself." With a celebration of the author's aesthetic in mind, Kenan walks his readers through the contents of the book—"Baldwin's essays, profiles, reviews, letters, introductions, and a short story" (xxiv)—works that attempt to mirror the broad experimentation with genre and tone that made James Baldwin such a famous intellectual.

In his reviews, he "comes across . . . as a pretty strict and unforgiving taskmaster," Kenan notes; he especially mentions his famous feud with Richard Wright over Baldwin's review of *Native Son* and Ross Lockridge Jr.'s suicide after a particularly vicious review of his novel *Raintree County.* But "Baldwin's letters, on the other hand, strike a more complex mélange of emotions" (xv), where the author can be both "fiery" and "longing" at the same time. The real focus of the collection, Kenan argues, are the long-form essays: "it is thrilling to see so many of these largely forgotten pieces reintroduced to wider circulation," he gushes (xxvii). One such piece—"Of the Sorrow Songs: The Cross of Redemption"—gives Kenan his title for the entire collection. In that essay, Baldwin celebrates the spirit of the blues as "our witness, and our ally" (xxvii).

Kenan concludes his introduction to the collection by thinking through the rhetorical strategies of students when confronted with Baldwin's philosophy: "What . . . would James Baldwin think of Barack Obama?" (xxix). Kenan divines the answer from a speech collected in the volume, one written for the Liberation Committee for Africa, where Baldwin imagines the possibility of the first "Negro President": "What I am really curious about," Baldwin explains in his speech, "is just what kind of country he'll be President of" (xxix). Some of the answers to the mystery of what it means to be James Baldwin might just be answered in this "timely volume," Kenan suggests, even if we value those mysteries above Baldwin's prodigious intellect.

### "Randall Kenan on *Ode to Billie Joe*" (2011)

Kenan's essay, published in a special issue of the journal *Southern Cultures* that focused on the role of the south in popular film, explores the film *Ode to Billie Joe* (1976).[10] Other contributions included Alice Walker's piece on *Cold Mountain,* Elizabeth Spencer's article on *The Reivers,* and Alan Gurganus writing on *Sherman's March*. In his opening, Kenan explains the movie's central aesthetic appeal: "This is Romeo and Juliet set in post–World War II rural Mississippi. Romeo is played by Robby Benson, 1976's version of the Jonas Brothers all wrapped up in one; Juliet being a doe-like Glynnis O'Connor, whom the camera loves" (33).

The movie is important partly because of its relation to the song that inspired it but also as "the first of a short run of memorable movies about the Dirty South, tinged with erotica and nostalgia" (33).

Kenan's memory of that south imbues the film with a personal and regional symbolism that even now, in his adult life, he cannot quite shake: "I saw it at a small theater in Wallace, North Carolina, when I was but thirteen. . . . It was the first movie I remember haunting me and actually causing a mild depression. Melancholy. I was too young to have a sense of surety (What did Billie Joe McAllister do to cause himself so much pain?); my notions were inchoate, and too vague even for a premonition. I probably knew the word 'homosexual,' but its meaning was but an urge in my pants and far from any reality. Yet what I am certain of now is the sense of dread, the Signs in the Sky, the warnings and omens, the pre-figuration of doom: Beware all ye who enter here. There be Dragons there, y'all!" (33).

*Ode to Billie Joe* did something to a young Randall Kenan that he cannot quite explain away as being the hallmark of an adolescent penchant for melodrama, even if the film was "so true to the adolescent spirit, lacking in all taste or any sense of proportion; so in love with its own melodramatic knowledge of being alive and of having feelings"; there is still something in the final scene, in which Billie Joe confesses his love and his unworthiness to his love, that lays Kenan bare: "I felt naked when I watched it, revealed, and feel naked even now when I see it," he concludes (34).

**"When We All Get to Heaven"** (2013)

Published in the spring issue of *The Virginia Quarterly Review,* Kenan's short story opens with Ed Phelps—the farmer who finds Clarence Pickett communing with buzzards in his field in Kenan's short story "Clarence and the Dead"—returning to New York City after having been away for thirty years.[11] Amid the din of the tourists and Rockefeller Center and the Carnegie Deli, Ed is in town with his wife, Isaline, "for the National Baptist Convention, being held at that very moment in the Javits Convention Center way, way over on 11th Avenue" (115). Isaline is there to attend as a delegate from Tims Creek and North Carolina, but her business trip allows Ed the opportunity to break free from his routine as a plumber and enjoy the sights and sounds of the city. Early on, Ed walks around, taking in the mix of culture he sees—both the high and the low (he watches a homeless man throw up and is given a card advertising "New York's Most Sophisticated Pussy").

We learn more and more about Ed as the story progresses. Walking and seeing all of New York's attractions, the fifty-eight-year-old father of three continues his ambling exploration, all the time "feeling fine," as Kenan reminds us. On the corner of 53rd Street, Ed runs into a mob of white teenagers waiting for someone—someone who turns out to be famous. The man watches as a white limousine pulls up and lets out a man with hair "all blond like hoar frost and needle-looking, like a porcupine, or like a man who had stuck his finger into a light socket and saw God all at the same time" (116–117). Caught up with the throng there to see the young man—who we find out later is Billy Idol—Ed gets taken backstage and is mistaken for a rhythm and blues legend by the name of the Deacon. Convinced that he is meeting one of his idols, Billy explains to his manager "a long, detailed story about how Ed/the Deacon had grown up on a plantation in Mississippi, and had run away to Memphis at the age of twelve, and how he had run into a great big chicken at the same crossroads as had Robert Johnson ('You do know who Robert Johnson is, don't you, darling? Yeah, I thought you might not.'), and how he got a recording contract with Sam Phillips and then Chess Records—and Ed Phelps couldn't keep up with the story but found it so very compelling that he wanted to hear this man's music until it hit him—making him laugh—that he was, indeed, this very man. Lord, this boy could tell a good lie. Ed more than halfway admired that" (118).

Caught in a case of mistaken identity, Ed does not know how to respond when Billy asks him to play. Although he finds the situation laughable, he does recognize the seriousness of the connection the two men are forming: "Two boys who together and without words recognize and acknowledge the Dangerous Thing, and, being like-minded, imagine assaying said Thing, and with each passing moment feel the Thing exert greater gravitational force upon the two, each to each, and along with the weight comes glee, anticipation, heat, so much so that the Dangerous Thing becomes the Irresistible Thing, the Inevitable Thing" (118).

Ed Phelps does, indeed, pick up Billy's guitar and play the one tune he remembers his father teaching him, a folk song about fishing. As he strums and sings, Ed notices "Billy's face was no longer cat-like, but all Christmas, and all the young people in the room were beaming and tapping their feet" (119), and when the song ends, all Billy can think of is how to work Ed/Deacon into his act on stage that night. Instead of inviting Ed onstage, Billy makes sure he has VIP access to the show. Ed's sense of astonishment and wonder is quickly deflated a bit by Billy's ridiculous performance: "It was silly music, it was loud music, it was all catchy phrases and easy beats, stuff he heard on the radio, and he figured he might have had to have heard some of this music on the radio in the past, but, to tell the truth, it all kinda sounded the same these days" (119). When Billy's manager comes to visit him in his VIP box, she tells Ed that she knows he is not really Deacon.

Billy insists on driving Ed back to his hotel; during their conversation, Ed learns that Billy brought him backstage for "a laugh" (120). Parting ways, Ed tells Billy his true identity, and he goes back to his wife, who bathes in the hotel room. As he waits for Isaline to finish her bath, Ed sees a music video on television with Billy singing about dancing with himself. He can't stand the song or the video, but seeing his new acquaintance on the screen thrills him a bit. Watching TV weighs Ed down, and he slowly drifts off to sleep thinking of singing and songs that mattered to him when he was a boy and remembering his grandfather: "the day turned to a guitar and the guitar strings turned to worms and the worms turned into cucumbers and the cucumbers turned into his mother's fingers, and she gave them to him peeled white with salt and pepper and a little vinegar, and the taste was childhood, and the taste was still new, and the sun was high in the sky, and it was 1946 and he was fourteen, and he was in the tobacco field, and deep in the lugs, and the day was hot, but he was happy—BACCOOO! BACCOOO! AIN'T NO BACCO IN HEAVEN I KNOW!—and he heard his grandfather's voice, and his grandfather was singing, and he heard his grandfather's voice and his grandfather was singing" (121).

Kenan's story has several hallmarks of the author's fiction, including meditations on the sacred and the profane (through the lens of music), the humor and pathos of simplicity in the face of complicated investments, an articulation of cross-generational anxiety that eventually flattens differences and draws people closer, and the power of narrative and stories to create and reimagine possibilities for growth and connection. Ed works for Billy Idol as a kind of go-between in a way that allows him to win a delicate power struggle with his producer, while Billy functions for Ed as a critical lens through which he can remember his childhood in a new and more vital way.

### *The Carolina Table* (2016)

In this recent collection published by Kenan's hometown press, Eno, the author assembles various narratives involving food from some of North Carolina's most famous writers.[12] Authors including Daniel Wallace, Jill McCorkle, and Lee Smith offer memories and stories involving food, while chefs such as Sophia Woo and Bill Smith write passionately about what food means to them. Kenan edited this anthology of North Carolina food writing, and in his introduction he explores the importance of food to him—both as an aesthetic for his writing and as a gateway to unlocking memories and personal meanings.

In "The Rooster, the Rattlesnake, and the Hydrangea Bush," Kenan goes back to his childhood in Chinquapin and to a certain feud he maintained with a rooster. Reminiscing, he asserts, "My childhood was not exactly idyllic, but I wouldn't trade it for Mark Zuckerberg's billions" (1), for Kenan's childhood world was full of food. His cousin Norman's farm contained the most delicious bounty: "a peach tree; a number of pear trees . . . and a grape arbor produc[ing] the plumpest, sweetest, purplest scuppernongs known to man or beast" (1–2).

Around from the scuppernong vine was a hydrangea bush that became part of a legend for Kenan when, while chasing a rooster, he almost got bitten by a rattlesnake that was so enraged it shook the entire bush to warn him of its impending attack. He concludes this section with a sentence that could be the epigraph to his entire fictional ethos: "My home, my world, was always edible. A moveable feast" (3).

Despite its stereotypical associations, Kenan finds the south to be an epicenter of thoughtfulness about food and foodways. His collection, he argues, tries to fight against the tired reworking of southern food as "folksy, old-fashioned, technophobic, churchified, photocopies of Mayberry and The General Lee" (5). Instead, Kenan wants to explore the complexity of North Carolina and its associations with food that move beyond fried stuff and barbecue, to talk about its bounty of sweet potatoes and blueberries and its nascent wine industry. "These connections are neither vague nor frivolous," he concludes, "but central to our state's character and the character of its people, even those who sincerely believe their lives are untouched by food they don't put in their mouths" (7).

In the final section of his introduction, Kenan waxes poetical on the subject of the DeKalb Farmer's Market, outside Atlanta, where one can find not only "the grains from Ethiopia, the nuts from Israel, the fruits from India and Malaysia, the fish from Europe, or the vegetables from Venezuela . . . but also . . . the people, this polyglot, multi-ethnic, multicolored parade of humanity coming together over one thing: food" (9). Kenan notes that the world of his native North Carolina is becoming more like the market, a shift that produces anxiety in some of its citizens—"What will happen to the old ways? they mutter. They see falafels as a threat; cactus pads as enemy combatants; sea cucumber as an arch invader" (9). But Kenan ends his introduction with an ode to this new, changing culinary landscape, dreaming aloud about "what blends and hybrids might occur, what new crops will we begin to grow, what new uses might we discover for sweet potatoes and tobacco plants and pine needles and the humble butter bean" (10).

# Afterword

## Randall Kenan Takes Flight

In the almost two years since the publication of *Understanding Randall Kenan,* one significant event occurred that necessitated an update: Kenan's short-story collection, *If I Had Two Wings,* was published in early August 2020; it is his first sustained work of fiction since the publication of *Let the Dead Bury Their Dead* in 1992. The collection garnered immediate acclaim. Kirkus reviews described it as "ten artful stories [that] conjure contemporary North Carolina, mouthwatering and matter-of-factly haunted." The *Chicago Review of Books* noted, "These stories are accomplished and polished . . . [Randall Kenan] successfully strikes a balance between fancy and finesse, arranging stories so that characters connect naturally and easily, which builds credibility and secures readers' engagement." Writing for *Slate,* Dan Kois compared the stories in *Two Wings* with those from *Let the Dead Bury Their Dead:* "The 10 stories in the new collection are as rich and provocative and funny as the ones that came before." In September, it was announced that *If I Had Two Wings* was on the longlist for the National Book Award; Kenan's *Let the Dead Bury Their Dead* was a National Book Award finalist in 1992.

Half the stories in *Two Wings* are either new or newly edited; the other half were previously published—of them, two were addressed in the hardback version of this book: "When We All Get To Heaven" (first published in the *Virginia Quarterly Review* in 2013) and "Now Why Come That Is?" (which first appeared in *Callaloo* in 1998). "Ain't No Sunshine" was published in *Black Renaissance/Renaissance Noire* in 2008, and "The Eternal Glory that is Ham Hocks" first appeared in *The Prairie Schooner*'s Winter 2012–2013 issue.

"Resurrection Hardware, or Lard & Promises" is the most recent, having been published in *The Oxford American*'s Spring 2018 issue. The stories in the collection stray in and out of Kenan's mythic Tims Creek, North Carolina, but even if they are not set directly in the town, they have a purposeful connection to Kenan's fictional postage stamp of soil.

The story "I Thought I Heard The Shuffle of Angel's Feet" begins with Cicero Cross broken down in Tims Creek in a Lexus that used to belong to his now-deceased lover, Jacson Ribeiro—whose book, *From Pixote, With Love,* briefly interrupts the flow of the narrative as Kenan quotes from it frequently. While waiting for AAA, Cicero is shocked when his old school friend, Tony Carter, instead rescues him. As the two reminisce, Cicero ponders his history with Tony, his visit to the town to sell his uncle Dax's land, and his tumultuous relationship with Jacson. Though they were acquaintances at Howard University, Jacson and Cicero did not develop a close friendship until they began working together on the same architectural project. They spent ten years together as lovers before Jacson died of AIDS. Now, after some time to process Jacson's death, Cicero begins to feel desire stirring inside of him, largely through revisiting his past with Tony. When Tony confesses that he has been HIV positive for seven years, his vulnerability entices Cicero to take a chance and kiss him full on the lips. Realizing he can't just leave Tony and his uncle the way he had intended, Cicero drives to Uncle Dax's retirement home and tells him he has decided not to sell the family land.

"The Eternal Glory that is Ham Hocks" is reminiscent of Kenan's "This Far" in *Let the Dead Bury Their Dead* in that an important historical figure comes to play a pivotal role in the lives of the residents of Tims Creek. In "This Far" that figure is Booker T. Washington, but in "Ham Hocks," it is tycoon Howard Hughes, who travels to Tims Creek to proposition a young African American woman, Inez Cross, to be his personal chef. Hughes is initially after Inez's mother, who, for a time, cooked for the Hughes family when Howard was a young man in Houston. At first perplexed by her Southern cuisine, Hughes is gradually charmed by it, especially her constant addition of ham hocks to flavor pots of beans. When he finds out that Inez's mother has passed, Hughes asks the young woman to move in with him and be his personal chef. Inez refuses, even though Hughes offers her a staggering amount of money. Turned off by Hughes's transactional views on labor—"I didn't like the smug way he asked. Like he could buy or sell folk on a whim"—Inez confesses to her son that she never even considered the idea. Like his mother, the nameless narrator son has become an accomplished chef; his restaurant in Los Angeles is famous for what critics call a "Nouvelle Soul Cuisine."

"Ain't No Sunshine" is something of a revenge tale for Kenan. Pastor Lazarus Barden II turns himself into the sheriff, an old school friend, Tony Cavanaugh, for attacking J. C. Stokes in the parking lot of the supermarket IGA. Lazarus's wife, Gina, had been Stokes's high school sweetheart until she discovered that he was cheating on her. After a quick marriage and an even-quicker divorce, Stokes pursues Gina once again. Despite warning signs, Lazarus chooses not to believe he is being made a cuckhold; however, a week before the attack, Stokes calls the house and tells Lazarus, "I wanna talk to my woman." Later, when Stokes confronts him on his way into the IGA by insulting him and demanding that he put Gina on the phone the next time he calls, Lazarus loses control, takes off his belt, and whips him brutally in the parking lot in front of a crowd of onlookers. The sheriff is amused by Lazarus's story, but concludes, "Sounds to me like that old fool had it coming."

Gloria Brown is the main character in the shortest story in the collection, "Ezekiel Saw the Wheel." She is preparing for her daughter, Tamar's, birthday party, which also doubles as a going-away party: Tamar is a master sergeant in the army who is about to leave for her third deployment. Gloria is haunted by a horrific nightmare in which Tamar dies in a helicopter, and Gloria's funeral-home job makes her gruesome thoughts worse. As she tries to console an out-of-towner whose wife suddenly dies of a massive stroke on their way to the Outer Banks, she finds her mind wandering to her recent dreams, Tamar's girlfriend, and what might happen if Tamar were to die overseas. When she realizes she has spent too long lost in her thoughts, she turns back to the man whose wife has died, and they share a long, meaningful gaze.

In "Mamiwata," Kenan explores the roots of Tims Creek. Set in the nineteenth century, the story follows thirteen-year-old Amanda—or Mandy as she is known to her family—and her Aunt Inez and Uncle Pharaoh—the founder of Tims Creek—as they hide from the "dogs and catchers" who are trying to capture runaway enslaved people. Mandy encounters a strange man in the middle of the creek; he can inexplicably summon catfish seemingly at will. At first distrustful of the strange but mystical man, Mandy is forced to decide between jumping into the water with him or being found by the catchers who are closing in on their encampment. In the final scene of the story, Mandy jumps in the water by the man and finds it warm, safe, and inviting.

In "Resurrection Hardware or, Lard & Promises," Kenan takes first-person narration and turns semiautobiographical. Unlike *Let the Dead Bury Their Dead,* this story's main character is "Randall Kenan"; the author's fictional avatar only appears in a footnote for the eponymous story in *Let the Dead Bury Their Dead*. The tale is something of a ghost story, beginning and ending with an apparition of a dark-skinned naked man who haunts an old farmhouse the narrator has purchased. Like Kenan, the narrator delivers lectures on Southern food, has moved back to North Carolina from New York City, and is openly gay. The Kenan narrator meets his lover, Siddiq, at a volunteer job in the Harlem Settlement House. Lured by his friend Alexa—whose idea for a Southern cooking magazine called "Lard & Promises" seems a perfect fit for him—the narrator and Siddiq move into the renovated farmhouse, where the narrator keeps seeing visions of the dark-skinned ghost as well as a mysterious White man with a hat who roams in the nearby cornfield. Doing some digging on the history of the house, the narrator learns that it was built in 1790 and became an inn run by Quakers. The docent at the Alamance County Historical Museum confides in Kenan: "I strongly believe that inn was used to smuggle slaves to freedom." During a particularly grisly encounter with a ghostly tableaux of dead people in his barn, Siddiq finally agrees that the farmhouse might be haunted, and at a party late one night, one of the guests confirms that he has also seen a naked man in the bathroom. In his Coda, Kenan confesses that Siddiq is not currently living with him, lured by the draw of the coast, but that his dark-skinned ghost is still in the house. Even though it is fall, when the narrator opens his door suddenly it is spring, and the White man from the cornfield appears in a boat. Kenan's "visitor, my new friend" steps down into the boat, and the man from the cornfield tells the narrator, "We need to get a-going. Seen two patrollers on horseback a few miles back." Though the boatman implores him to come with them, the narrator tells them he feels safe where he is. Eating breakfast alone, the narrator finds his mind wandering: "I think of my mother, I think of my lover, I think of home."

In one of the longer stories of the collection, "The Acts of Velmajean Swearington Hoyt and the New City of God," Kenan mixes religious meditation with *The Twilight Zone.* The story opens on Velmajean in her house surrounded by news vans and camera crews anxious to interview her. Everyone has come because Velmajean has somehow gained the power to perform miracles. It all started when, loading her car at the supermarket, Velmajean is approached by a young man who helps her with the bags. The dark-skinned man is oddly dressed in a long coat, and he tells her, "You are blessed among women . . . truly blessed." When he touches her hand, she feels a warmth that increases exponentially. Twenty minutes later Velmajean comes across a car crash and raises a little girl from the dead. Later during a Thanksgiving-in-May homeless food drive, Velmajean feeds hundreds of people even though she only has two trays of food. She performs so many miracles that she must call in private security to protect her from the throngs of those who wish to be healed. As she prepares for a live telecast manifesting one of her miracles, the young man from the supermarket crashes through her window, and Kenan offers us four different possibilities for an ending from different "gospels" of Velmajean's life. In each instance, the man tries to attack Velmajean with a knife and is either shot or wrestled to the ground by guards. As Velmajean approaches him, he confronts her with a terrifying question about her new powers: "Who said it was from God?"

The final story, "God's Gonna Trouble the Water, or Where is Marisol?" Kenan's main character, Mrs. Streeter, is in Barbados with her niece Desiree, a college freshman at Spellman. At the same time a hurricane approaches Barbados, one is hitting Streeter's hometown of Tims Creek. Unable to go back home because of the storm damage, Streeter and Desiree fly back to the states and stay with her son, Aaron, while they listen to the reports of the damage from the category 5 hurricane. She tries to get in touch with Marisol, a young woman that had helped her with housework, but she cannot seem to locate her. When she eventually is allowed home, Streeter finds devastation everywhere. She sets to work trying to clean up the place but cannot shake her anxiety over Marisol's sudden vanishing. She goes to a local store, "La Michoacanita Tienda Mexicana," rumored to sell the best pork chops in the state; however, no one seems to remember Marisol. Eventually the community rebuilds, and Streeter gets a heartbreaking letter from Sonya Ruiz, a woman who knew Marisol; she writes that Marisol lost her little daughter in the flood and returned to Chihuahua thanks to the owner of La Michoacanita. However, the entire family is missing, presumed kidnapped by "wicked men." She closes her letter asking Streeter to pray for the family. After a restless night of dreams, Streeter awakens and decides to visit the store, thinking "this would be a great day for pork chops."

*If I Had Two Wings* shares many of the themes and preoccupations found throughout Kenan's oeuvre: the magical intimacy of breaking bread; the mystery and majesty of foodways; the disarticulation of spirituality from purely religious sources; an unflinching examination and celebration of the profane. But the collection also deepens and expands Kenan's previous works by focusing on the themes of migration and flight. The book takes its title from a traditional song that celebrates the mystery of flying away from a world intent on doing one harm, and winged imagery abounds. And yet, Kenan also connects the need to fly away to a yearning desire to come to rest. Many of the characters in the book migrate away from Tims Creek—either mentally, emotionally, or physically. But all of them—including the "Randall Kenan" of "Restoration Hardware"—find themselves magnetically drawn back home. In some ways, this collection is a fitting conclusion to Kenan's profound experiment with Tims Creek. Because no matter how confining and frustrating one's home is, Kenan seems to suggest that the magic of place is forever etched into our soul. Kenan's *If I Had Two Wings* fulfills the promises made by *A Visitation of Spirits* and *Let the Dead Bury Their Dead* by finalizing a fictional triptych of a space as rich and compelling as those crafted by any American author.

# APPENDIX A

## *Writing B(l)ack: An Interview with Randall Kenan*

The following interview with Randall Kenan took place in December 2016 in Chapel Hill, North Carolina. My thanks go to Mr. Kenan and the University of Alabama's CARSCA Grant Committee, which supported my trip to interview the writer, as well as to Linda Angell, who edited the transcription of our conversation.

JAMES A. CRANK: I want to start by asking you to respond to something you wrote about your desire to write at an early age. You once wrote that, as a young man, you imagined writing as a way for you to "write back" on the page to the authors you were reading. What did you want to say to those early authors?

RANDALL KENAN: Poe seems so tangible, I think, because [the writing] is so old. And it was very much a nineteenth-century, eighteenth-century view of America. And that was where I was growing up in a strange sort of way. So, it got to me even though the language—I mean now when I go back and look at Poe's language I appreciate it. It can be rococo. Not *Tell-Tale Heart;* that is actually pretty straightforward. But I think, I was talking back to that vision, which is drenched in Christ and iconography of church and the Protestant Church in particular, some Catholicism if you swing that way, but it was very American Gothic, which is what I grew up to be.

JAC: When you were reading those stories, when you were reading Poe for example, did you see yourself in any of those characters? Did you sense your absence? Or was it just an escape?

RK: I don't know if escape is the right term. I mean I know how, that's a loaded term in my book. I would see myself in these things as Caliban, and I didn't understand it that way at the time. But that was the psychology behind it. And I'm trying to think—were there any of those figures in Poe in particular?

In Robert Louis Stevenson, there were plenty. And in Melville, but I can't think of anyone in particular in Poe.

JAC: Was the dark juvenilia you wrote a form of imitation?

RK: It was a form of play, and because it was so isolated, and because I loved the reading so much, it was a way of writing what you wanted to read. I think a part of play is imitation, and extension, and creation. Creation of a desirable thing. And practice.

JAC: Did you show them to anyone? Did you guard them?

RK: I didn't; because they were self-emanated I didn't really think they were particularly special. I would sort of do my own little documentary, put them in special places, maybe copy them over, that sort of thing—thinking that they would be special to me at some point at some level. But I never was into sharing them until much later. I mean I would write little plays and things that were to be performed, but they were in no way autobiographical or self-expressive. Certainly not the things I was interested in at the time.

JAC: As you matured as a writer at university, you were encouraged by several professors to abandon science fiction and magical realism, and yet you still clearly wrote stories with elements of fantasy and magic in them. What did/does magic realism and the supernatural offer you as a resource to think about your fiction?

RK: Well I was an ornery cuss, and I was listening to them with two ears. "Okay, I hear what you're saying. I'm going to do what I want to do and I'm going to find a way to do what I want to do." Well, again, it goes back to that bedrock of what spoke to me about Poe and all that, which was: folklore—and even theology and religion—are fantastical, on some level. When you tell the Jesus story verbatim: this kid from Palestine who's really smart and tells all the priests and wise men stuff that they don't know, and goes on and on and on, and changes water into wine one day, and walks on water, and brings people back from the dead: that's really magical. That's sort of the height of it. And all that book is just chocked full of it. I mean there's no technology, but Augustin tells us that miracles are just technology we don't understand. And that's a great rubric for understanding science fiction. I think it does what narrative does best, which is translate the world into metaphors that we manipulate much more easily in our animal brain. Once I found the [Latin] Boom writers and started reading writers like Zora Neale Hurston, I found more acceptable masks for [my stories]. And it seemed, the higher degree of teachers like Daphne Athas and Doris Betts [understood them]; I found some other professors who were noncreative writing teachers who encouraged me as well. So, I kind of broke through that.

JAC: Teachers in science and physics, for example?

RK: My physics advisers suggested that was what I was all about. And, at the time, I think I might have approached it differently then, but, at the time, it seemed so remote. The only black [science] fiction writer was Samuel Delaney. Octavia Butler was publishing, but nobody knew who she was. And most of them didn't know either of them were black. Delaney never hid it, but his publisher didn't go out of his way to show pictures of him. And he was married to a white woman, and that would have been just too much. Then he came out as gay. Octavia Butler, it took her a long time; she was publishing in the 1970s, but it wasn't until *Kindred* started getting on people's syllabuses and she won the MacArthur genius before people knew her.

JAC: What did your career as an editor help you with as you considered your role as a fiction writer? What kind of practical help did it offer you?

RK: I used to call it my graduate school, but now that I know more about graduate school, it was my apprenticeship. It demystified the whole publishing industry and took away a lot of anxieties about what it really is. I think for unpublished young people, they are surrounded by this sort of, not only a mythology and a romance but a sort of magic. There's something supernatural about it. There ain't nothing supernatural about it. It's business. And what I fell in love with about publishing was the minutia, the different stages one goes through in publishing a book, both physically and in terms of marketing and getting the word out, the publicity, all that sort of thing. That was an education, and demystifying that much of it, I think, made me re-entrench my technical sense of the word and putting things down.

JAC: Did it also teach you not to be so precious with your writing in some respects?

RK: There you go. Seeing the better writers—and it became almost a truism, the better writers enjoyed and appreciated being edited more than the lesser writers. The lesser writers were the ones who would sort of bitch and scream. And say, "Oh no, I'm not changing that word. That sentence was so goddamn wonderful you put it back you," you know. And the good writers would say, "Okay we'll just cut this whole page, or we'll cut this whole chapter." Tom Wolfe tells this story of the book he wrote after *A Man in Full,* where he came to New York to have dinner with Jonathan Galassi. He had brought the nine-hundred-page manuscript, and during this lunch, he realized that he'd screwed up. So, he said, "Jonathan, I'm going to do you a favor. I'm not going to give you this book. I'm going to give you the first 150 pages of this book and the rest I'm just going to get rid of." At that level . . . talk about not being precious. How can you not be precious with 750 pages?

JAC: You had written an early version of *Visitation of Spirits* when you were at the University of North Carolina at Chapel Hill. How did that novel begin, and how did it evolve through the process of editing?

RK: I had the overarching vision, let's put it that way, of developing a place and the place having some sort of deep, deep, deep, roots, and to be, as Flannery O'Connor said, "Christ-haunted." The early book, there was lycanthropy, and the character would be Horace Cross as a lawyer coming back to North Carolina. And there he got into some mischief, and was cursed, and turned into a werewolf. It was such an adolescent plot. It was an adolescent story, and when I moved to New York—first, I moved to New Jersey, and I lived with relatives for a few years—and that's when it came to me. I was working in publishing, and I said, "I got this whole thing bass ackwards. I should be writing from someone who's not so much older than me, but someone who's younger than myself." And lycanthropy, I'm writing about it because it's sexy, but what I'm really interested in is what is more, you know, that's haunted me most of my life. Haunted. Demon possession. And so that sort of came together at the same time.

JAC: Was the process of getting *Visitation* ready a sort of coalescing—because the structure of *Visitation* is so strong. I'm wondering, during this time, when you're editing *Visitation,* and you're also working as an editor, was this all planned? Or did you have in your mind this is going to now be the structure?

RK: No, and thank you for the compliment on structure because that's my math and science background. I was recently with a friend in New York, and she showed me a manuscript [of an early version of *Visitation of Spirits*]. It was so much more free-form, and some things about it I really admired. But I'd forgotten it. It was ancient history. I think after I'd done that really early draft, it sort of vomited out all the things you need to vomit out, I realized it needed more structure, and so I came up with this very complex four-part quadripartite. But it was going to have four parts instead of three parts that sort of interwove, and I realized it's going to be one hell of a long book. It's going to be one hell of a complicated book—the kind of book I would like to read, but I don't know if anybody else is going to want to read it. And also young and impatient, so I eschewed the fourth part and that became the end of *Let the Dead Bury Their Dead*.

JAC: When you were actually able to get this book out, I am curious about your expectations and then what the response did to those expectations. I'm thinking not just of critics but of your family and of your community, too.

RK: Well, those are two different things. Remember, I had done my apprenticeship at one of the premiere houses in the country. I had absolutely no expectations. I knew, because I had published books at that point, that a first novel's chance in this world was like a canoe's chance in the Atlantic, you know. And that's probably more accurate than it sounds. I had absolutely no expectations of it doing anything. I was just happy to get a book published, and I was looking on to the next thing. So, I was not crushed when I didn't get any airtime review. I was happy to be reviewed by the *Chicago Tribune*. Because I had no expectations, that was like, "Ohhhhhh, thank you Jesus!" And the biggest thing, the biggest success of that book at the time was, I think, a month or two after it came out. Anchor Books paid me a fairly substantial amount for then, for a young editorial assistant, for the paperback rights. One of my mentors in my apprenticeship, the great vice president of advertising Nina Bjorn—her office was a few doors down from mine—and, in all my exuberance, I rushed in, I said, "Nina, Nina, Anchor Books just paid me $20,000 for paperback rights." And she said, "Oh no dear, that's a disaster. Your first novel should be a disaster." I didn't realize I was coming out in that book, and it was completely self-denial, because—I remember the moment: I was with a friend of mine. I was standing on the platform of the E train, waiting for the F train, and it sort of came to me. I sort of said that [I was coming out in this novel] to him, and he looked at me: "What the hell's wrong with you? Of course! Are you just getting this? What were you thinking all this time?"

JAC: That's my question about your family—because on the one hand you published this book, you're a legitimate superstar, right? For your family, anything that you do that's on the national level, that's going to be read as the hugest success ever. And yet it was also very personal, a very personal novel. So how did they deal with that?

RK: They didn't. I think I was protected somewhat (A) because it didn't become *The Help,* and everybody was not talking about it. It didn't become a movie. Then I would have been in trouble. And it's not a superliterate world out there. I think my mother read it. I think some of my cousins read it, and they—because they were literate—they were probably more open-minded. I had one cousin who was a minister who I didn't know very well, and he became very morose as if he had failed me in some way. But they didn't really talk about my writing seriously until the second book. And then there was "Cornsilk," oh shit!

JAC: Publishing that book allowed you to do a lot of things: One of them was it allowed you to change your profession, to teach. That had to have changed your process for writing or even thinking about yourself as a writer. When you're an editor, you're sort of in the trenches—there are a lot of different responsibilities you have. Now you're a professor, it's got to allow you a little bit more freedom in terms of writing?

RK: Theoretically. I think having to work so hard in publishing forced me to work harder at writing, because I couldn't take any time for granted. I was writing on subways. I read this thing about V. S. Naipaul. He would work after he graduated from Oxford; he got a job writing copy for the BBC. And his first couple of books, he would stay after he finished the BBC's work and work on his own work at the same typewriter. And that's the sort of romance that appeals to me. And so I started doing that while working in publishing; I would—when everybody was gone, I'd go out, have a sandwich, come back, and start doing my own work. And that kind of rigidity doesn't exist when you teach two classes a week and you're not making as much money—where there's more time to get in trouble. And to read, which is necessary. I think the positive thing was being forced to think about art in some more systematic way, which already appealed to me. But getting myself away from all these gray beards who knew what they knew and weren't going to explain why—oh, I'm not going to buy this book and give you a few words about it. I had time to sort of tear it apart, figure it out.

JAC: Obviously, the last story in *Let the Dead Bury Their Dead* was supposed to be the final section of *Visitation*. Are there other ways beside setting and characters that you find your two book-length works connected?

RK: Everything pre-1993–1994, which was analog, most of [those drafts] were lost in all my moves. I moved so much and I couldn't keep a hold of everything, but I was very much enamored of Robert Calasso's *The Lineage of Cadmus and Harmony,* which sort of takes the whole family—and it goes back before that because I think it starts with Europa and the bull and all that. And I had this ambition to create that sort of radiance of these people, and I still do in a way. I wrote an essay about Baldwin and his great unwritten novel, and he was going to do this sort of thing. And there was a Brazilian novel that did it, called *An Invisible Memory,* which takes a family all the way back to Northwest Passage and all the way up to current history, but it's so hard. Also, I became more interested in the granular story.

JAC: So much of *Let the Dead Bury Their Dead* is microscopic, and the stories get really, really, really narrow—for example, focusing on one person's intimate relationship. Is that what happened? You were thinking about this grand thing, but you ended up going really small?

RK: Right, right, and that's what the Modernists taught us anyway. I'm a great student of Modernism. But those authors exist in that backdrop, so the possibility is always there. And the work is always informed in the same way that Euripides and Aristophanes and all these guys were influenced by the great story. And that's how you get that wonderful form *Leda and the Swan* by Yeats. Fantastic poem. That poem doesn't exist without that knowledge.

JAC: There were only three years between the publication of *Visitation* and the appearance of *Let the Dead Bury Their Dead*. How did you know the second collection was ready? Did you want it to be a novel, too?

RK: I am very sensitive about being told when to turn stuff in—I think I've even gotten worse. And that's what took me so long with *Walking on Water.* My agent at the time, Eric Ashworth, could tell me, "Okay, you need to get this done now, son." I had a great deal of respect for him, for Eric. I was lucky, I had spent the summer of 1990 at McDowell Coffey. I got a lot of it written there. I was still working on it when, I guess it was back when *Visitation* was coming out? I was on the road, I was heading out to start researching *Walking on Water,* and I was still working on some of those stories. I turned in a story that Elaine did not like, and so I said, "Okay, I have this Booker T. Washington story in my head"—which I wrote totally in a borrowed apartment room and motel, but I had been cooking that story for a long time. I had imbibed Louis Harlan's two-volume biography of Booker T. Washington. I had read *Up from Slavery* and other bits and pieces, doing research on Tuskegee. So, I knew I was ready to write it. I just had wanted to write about it. I felt bad about Percy Terrell. I felt I'd done bad things to him in all the other stories. I wanted to write a story that redeemed him. So the first story I did that redeemed him didn't redeem him. So everything else had been completed except for that.

JAC: So you knew very quickly, this wasn't going to be a novel. You weren't working on like a second novel?

RK: No.

JAC: You knew the structure was going to be a collection of short stories tied around Tims Creek?

RK: And Elaine bought it that way. I sold that at the same time I sold *Walking on Water.* And she bought it as a collection of stories. It was a two-book deal. And those stories had already been written. And she makes fun of me to this day about it—I wanted thirteen stories in that collection.

JAC: Why did she make fun of you?

RK: Thirteen.

JAC: Lucky number thirteen.

RK: Right. Silly man.

JAC: I think it's fair to say that when that collection came out, your life changed dramatically, right? Not just the fact it became such a critical success with the nomination for the National Book Award, but the collection allowed you opportunities financially. You got a lot of awards. You could travel. You had a lot more resources. How did you handle that? How do you handle success like that?

RK: I was fortunate in one way, in that I'd already been teaching. And I had this contract for a nonfiction book. Alice Hoffman said that her thing is to always have books under way when you get the galleys from the last project—which is a lot of pressure. It's too intense. But it does help focus the mind.

JAC: Is that when your family starts taking notice? Or your community?

RK: I mean it got a lot more fuss. People started showing up in Chinquapin and asking, and calling on the phone. I was at the National Book Awards ceremony with Robert Stone, Richard Price, Joyce Carol Oates. I can't remember. It's still too heady. That was the year that *Lincoln from Gettysburg* won and he was there. Garry Wills. There was a dinner for that award. That's the National Book Award. This is at a suite in the Time/Life building.

JAC: You also kind of became—and I think this is moving into your work on *Walking on Water*—a bit of a public intellectual, certainly a literary critic of some merit. How did you balance that role of fiction writer, professional writer, with your emerging role as public intellectual and literary critic?

RK: Well, I wanted it. I actually thought I wanted it. I came to New York, and that's what I wanted to do. George Bernard Shaw—I read very carefully how he had tried to do it. And I knew that there was going to be very little sleep involved. And, also, since I'd been running away from Baldwin so hard up until that point, of course everything I ran to was stuff that Baldwin did: he had been reviewing from the very start before *The Nation*. And so when *The Nation* called me up—just like Lena Horne, I never know how to say no. She says, there's a line in her show, "I never know how to say no to the right people." So I would get invited to do things, and I would say, "Okay, I'll do it."

JAC: Very soon after the excitement over *Let the Dead Bury Their Dead*, that biography of Baldwin comes out. I know meeting Baldwin in Chapel Hill was sort of a foundational experience: were you thinking about that moment for a long time, or was it more like you had completed your books and now were ready to turn to Baldwin and start to understand him and his life? Why, at that moment, Baldwin?

RK: I had always been afraid that it could happen. I had always been, in a way, preparing for it, and I think Martin Duberman knew it: one of the last projects I worked on at Knopf was the authorized biography of Baldwin. I'd worked with Duberman on his massive biography of Paul Robeson. So some of it is organic in that sense, in the way that things in New York publishing work. You know a guy who knows a guy.

JAC: Is it fair to say that Baldwin's more of an influence on your nonfiction than he is on your fiction? Or do you even think about those things?

RK: I think about them. I mean I still think highly of a lot of his fiction, and I have gotten into, not fights, but discussions, with Trudier Harris about *Just*

*Above My Head*. Because of what I think. I keep trying to redeem it. She won't let me.

JAC: I have to ask about *Walking on Water,* because it seems like such a tremendous undertaking. How in the world did you ever envision this project? Some of it has to be youthful exuberance and not really understanding the scope of the project? Is that fair to say?

RK: Oh, unavoidable. Unavoidable. My greatest disappointment and my greatest celebration in a way, but yeah, I was in there with two things: One was William Least Heat-Moon, *Blue Highways*. That was a huge deal when I was in high school. Nobody even knows it now. When I was in high school that was a huge book. It was a sort of quintessential Americana, because what he did was he updated *Travels with Charlie,* which I had no idea until well after *Walking on Water* was published, that people questioned why Steinbeck did half the shit he did. That was with *Travels with Charlie,* but I came fresh out of Chinquapin, and I believed it. That happened. Dammit. Don't question. They did that shit. I'm going to do it. And I'd just read Naipaul's *A Turn in the South*. Sonny Mehta walked into my office with the manuscript. He said, "You're from the South, tell me what you think of this." And I—you know I'm thinking, "Well, hell, I can do better than this."

JAC: Is it fair to say that *Walking on Water* is writing back against Naipaul in the way that you were writing back on the page to Beatrix Potter and Robert Louis Stevenson or Edgar Allan Poe? Because, in some ways, *Walking on Water* seems to speak through so many of the silences that Naipaul ignored in *A Turn in The South*.

RK: Well, it was so fresh in my mind. And he had always loomed large; I was interested in doing more of that type of writing, so it's hard to say no. And then he ends in Chapel Hill. So, at the same time that *Blue Highways* got huge, I fell in love with the human voice and the idea of presenting it in that way.

JAC: Was this fun? I mean, was going out and doing this enjoyable? Or did it become tedious, like doing this traveling, collecting these stories? Did anything surprise you? Maybe you thought it was going to be one way, but it turned into something else?

RK: After nine months, it got a little old. And that's when I switched how I was doing it. I mean I made a big dramatic sweep about coming home, and I felt like I failed because I was going to go out like William Least Heat-Moon, in one fell swoop and just sort of eat the whole country, you know? Very Hunter S. Thompson of me, but I'm no Hunter S. Thompson. And then I would go out in subsequent summers, and I think after the third summer, I just didn't want to meet anybody more—the idea of going through another transcription. And it feels uncompleted because of that, because only people who have read it all the way through, which is very few I know of, but they know I started two or three motifs. One was going to barbershops, and that just stopped. The other one was black men who were into *Star Trek*. And I wanted to end up—this is when I was in Mississippi sort of doing the final revision—at this huge *Star Trek* Convention in Long Island. And that turned that into sort of a personal thing. But I just couldn't do it.

JAC: Well, I tell you the book reminds me a lot of *Let Us Now Praise Famous Men*. Agee was writing an impossible story that he realized in the midst of collecting the narrative that he couldn't even begin to tell. I mean, is part of the project failure?

RK: It's interesting you mention Agee, because I read Lawrence Bergreen's biography on him. He spends a lot of time talking about him working on *Famous Men* and all of the moving about. I remember thinking, "Oh my God. I can't let this happen to me." You know, I guess I didn't get beat up as much he did [by his editors].

JAC: I'm wondering about biting off so much and if you actually thought, "Well, I'm going to accomplish understanding American blackness by going all across America. And when I get back, there will be some sort of conclusion to all of this?" And you didn't really get there, right?

RK: I don't think so. I mean, all these great books loom over one's head—you think of it as hopeful, and that was one of the models. Studs Terkel kept writing the same thing over and over. He came up with a book called *Race*. He came out with a book called *Will the Circle Be Unbroken*. He wrote a book after that. He's in his nineties. But it's just a hard project *altogether.*

JAC: Did you ever think about it becoming multimedia? A project with photographs?

RK: I talked to my agent about it at the beginning and he mentioned Agee and Terkel: they have pictures. He said, "You don't need pictures," and I let him convince me. This was well before Internet and all that sort of thing.

JAC: You've been working on this second novel for a while—it has had a number of different titles. But now, it feels like you've settled on, *There's A Man Going 'Round Taking Names*. Where are you with this new project? Can you talk about just the process of writing that novel and why it's taking a little bit of time?

RK: The last time I changed the title, because this hasn't been an easy iteration, because it was originally *The Fire and the Baptism,* which I'm not as enamored with, but when I published the *Fire This Time,* I realized I couldn't come up with a book right after that called something so similar. Too many fires. I had to put out one of the fires. But I was already in love with this spiritual, and what happened was, I saw this British film which starts with this old Negro spiritual—and somebody who I thought was Marian Anderson, because of the time, the setting, between the two great wars. I'd been asking scholars, "Where is this Marian Anderson recording singing *There's A Man Going 'Round Taking Pictures*?" And there's no such Marian Anderson recording. All this time I knew there was a version by Jessye Norman, but I thought it was Marian Anderson. The movie's been out of print for decades. On Sundance they show it one night, and I think—goddamn, that's Jessye Norman, not Marian Anderson! The album came out in the '70s. So, I chose that, and it kinda resonates: because there's a theme of kidnapping and body snatching. And I found out so much about the history of Chapel Hill—especially the university medical school. It explores the idea that the university used, for gross anatomy, black bodies. And the history of how they got those black bodies is a rather dark and buried secret.

JAC: Is it a historical novel—how would you characterize it?

RK: More historical than not.

JAC: Where are you in that process?

RK: Ummmm, I feel I shouldn't tell you this. I've taken some time off to finish this thing I started in Texas, the ghost story? But it was kind of an emotional thing to do it. To stop and start working on this, but I would sort of pick up and write on it. It sort of possessed me, if you will. And I realized, well, hell, I'm almost done with it. And maybe that'll get my agent off my back. I turn it in next week.

JAC: Is it a misnomer to say that a lot of your fiction is autobiographical? Like you're wrestling with a lot of complicated issues: the setting, first of all, which clearly references Duplin county and Chinquapin and all that stuff; a lot of your characters have things that happen to them that are similar to what happened to you: is that fair?

RK: I would pick at that a little bit. 'Cause I think what people mean when they say that is—you know, this is like, a transcript of what actually happened. And maybe I changed the names a little bit. But I tinkered a lot more.

JAC: A lot of *Visitation* feels hyperpersonal, and I know it's not a transcription, but you were struggling with a lot of issues about your sexual identity. That's fair to say, right?

RK: Yeah.

JAC: Is it hard to write about that? Is it hard to access that?

RK: Not all the time. I mean, I think I was distanced enough from it at the time that the difficulty for me is the embarrassment that attends that sort of self-revelation. You know, like, "Ooh, shit, I shouldn't read what people say about this." That leads to a certain discomfort, but I think part of the thing that appealed to me about writing is that when you're in the minutia of it, when you're in the sentences and the commas and the tenses and the grammars and all that stuff, you would get distracted from what seemed so there and immediate. It becomes this sort of setting down and cleaning it up and—there's an outside chance.

JAC: Your fiction feels like it's more of a working through of voices. Is that right? That you're trying to find different voices? Maybe voices from your past. Maybe voices that you invented, and in some way then, all that writing feels personal because it's all interior. Would that be fair to say?

RK: I would be lying if I said it wasn't. Although I think that the word "autobiographical," because it is not, you know, a direct putting down of what happened, but it does deal with a lot of what one has lived through. And also, and this is a cliché, I think writers do it too often. A lot of the most autobiographical characters are not the ones who have a direct or one-to-one correspondence with somebody like me. It might be a woman. It might be an old man. It might be a white dog.

JAC: One of the things that *Visitation* works through so beautifully is this negotiation between the spiritual world, religion, and these very obvious and carnal, bodily impulses that Horace is going through, as in adolescence, that feel to him antithetical to the religious world that he's experiencing. Is this something that you are actually trying to tease out, this body/mind split, and, if so, was making Horace an adolescent one of the main reasons for that? In *Ashes Don't Burn,* was Horace an older character?

RK: He was a young kid. No, no, he was in his twenties. A lawyer. He graduated from law school and was working as a lawyer. When you said that, I was thinking about how, when I was a little younger than Horace, I was interested in Egyptian mythology and archeology. I think King Tut's funeral was traveling then. That made me interested in Egyptian stuff, and I was reading all these stories. And there's this thing in Egyptian mythology about the Ka in the Ba. Apparently, they were one of the first cultures to separate the physical from the spiritual. Was that why I chose his name as Horace? Who's wanting to turn himself into a hawk? I don't know. I think I'm too intelligent not to have a plan, but the first time I actually said that was in a class last week. I'd never made that connection before. About Horace. I think I knew on some level. Why I abandoned making that, I don't know. I think that I thought it was too cheesy.

JAC: But sometimes you do surprise yourself—like, "Is that why I did that? I'm a clever person."

RK: Yeah, but the Ka-Ba thing is there. And the body and the soul, I think that goes hand in hand with the whole idea that we're talking about: why have we been coming back to spirit possession over and over again? Why is that so compelling to us?

JAC: Did anyone ever approach you about making movies or television shows, or any of that stuff?

RK: People nibbled at *Let the Dead Bury Their Dead,* but I swear, it was one show that ripped it off. A woman who audited a class I taught at Columbia called me up and said that she was working for a production company at CBS, and they wanted to adapt/work on adapting *Let the Dead Bury Their Dead*. But they didn't want to pay any money, and my agent said well. . . . And Parker Stevenson's company came out a year later with "American Gothic"—where there's this kid and there's a ghost and a guy who talks to a sheep, I think, instead of a hog. And I talked to my agent, who said, "Well, we can't do anything about it because they made them white and the American legal system is so racist." That's all they have to do is say, "Well, these are white characters. These aren't black characters."

JAC: If someone, a student, say, encounters your fiction for the first time, one of the things that they'll think is that you play around a lot with forms of narration and genre—suddenly breaking into screenplay, or drama, in the middle of *Visitation of Spirits;* the kind of lyric openings and closings that you have in that novel; the epistolary forms—you play around a lot with those hybridized forms of narration and genre. Why do you do that?

RK: I think it comes off to me as play. And it excites me along that level. I think for some odd reason of Manuel Puig's *Kiss of the Spiderwoman;* it was an exuberant thing. It was like, "You can't do this! What are you doing? What are you doing?" It just excited me on that level. "How the hell did you get away with that?" And it was fun. And I think I was working as a desk clerk. So, I was reading late into the night, and it kept me awake. So, I mean if it can do that, it'll keep your adrenaline pumping at three o'clock in the morning.

JAC: And that part of *Visitation* where the break comes is such a visceral and important part; it makes it more vital somehow to that story. It feels like it's so important that you have to step out of the bounds of narration or form. I mean, was that conscious? Now this is an important part, I'm going to highlight this?

RK: Well, I think that informs why I chose to do it there, and the other time I chose to do it at a Thanksgiving dinner, I think. And they're inherently dramatic. And if I had written them in scenes, they would have felt kind of like regular fiction.

JAC: You have this way of articulating a magic that comes from cross-generational intimacy, usually among men—that men of one generation to another generation, when they share something, there's an intimacy that's created.

And it performs a kind of magic. I'm thinking about "Clarence and the Dead" and "When We All Get to Heaven," where men of different generations form an intimacy, and it's transformational in some way. Did you have strong intimacies with people older than you as you were growing up?

RK: Oh, that sounds beautiful. I hope it's true. I would love for it to be true. It would surprise me that it's not something that everyone experiences, but you don't sound skeptical.

JAC: Especially among men; it feels like, once men reach a certain age, there's no more manufacturing of intimacy unless it's in their age group. And I think that's so untrue and that there is something in your stories where transformation and evolution happen. When you were growing up, were your closest friends of different generations?

RK: I think that would be safe to say. Yeah. I mean, again, you're in a fairly isolated place, so there weren't a lot of—you know, I went to school with people my age, but when I came back home, it was usually older people.

JAC: Did you feel like an old soul when you were growing up, you know?

RK: I always feel eighty years old when I say that.

JAC: Taking "When We All Get to Heaven": the magic that seems to come from that story is this chance kind of encounter; it's not just celebrity, but it's an intimacy that gets manufactured suddenly in a moment. And it's transformational in very small ways. And I think a lot of it happens because these are two men crossing a line of generation. But in your other fiction, you work through crossing all kinds of lines—generations, class, race, time, religion. Are you celebrating the magic of intimacies when you cross these lines?

RK: Well it probably comes up over and over again. You wonder, "Have I written the same novel over and over again?" I think it's possible. I think it's underestimated, and it's something about people: I think it takes a certain kind of person who's willing to play like that. To extend themselves. And it's something of a dance, a metaphor for intimacy. That they're willing to dance with each other. And let go of a certain fear and not be so guarded. If you're too guarded, you won't be able to achieve that. And I see it happening, and it's a beautiful thing when it does. But it's rare when it happens. I think that's why you prize it so much when it does.

JAC: You're lumped together with magic realism, supernatural, and fantasy, but really the thing that you're tethering your fiction to is the transformational nature of intimacy. And that can be the most mundane thing in the world: intimacy between two people. Especially men. Can you talk a little bit about queerness as a vehicle for storytelling?

RK: Hmmmmm. I need a definition of queerness, because I got in trouble at VONA, Voices of Our Nations, where I taught the LGBTQIA workshop, which was an education. The language moves so rapidly, and you have to task yourself to keep up. The whole idea of cisgender, right? Because there was a student whom I referred to as "Mrs.," thinking I was being polite and respectful. But she came up to me afterwards and told me quite bluntly, that she did not have a gender and she didn't appreciate me having gendered her and in front of the whole class. I probably said, "I'm so sorry, Miss." But I made a number of other mistakes, I sent them samples to discuss in class that were not by people of color or openly gay people. And that was a big no-no. They wanted those voices. So, I had to start over again, and I gave them excerpts from *Sonata Mulattica* after we had gone through some more canonical material. Proper canonical material for that setting. And the question was: this is Rita Dove. It's about a black violinist in Beethoven's Germany: is this queer enough for you? Because this feels really queer to me. And they all agreed with me. So, that's why I'm interested in the definition of what queering is. I think it is more than just that expression of gender or sexuality that runs against the norm. But it is transgressional. It is oppositional. And it's movable, too.

JAC: Can we talk about the dichotomy between an individual and their community, any kind of community—a religious community, family, school, a generation? I want to think about belonging to that community as both empowering on the one hand and limiting and claustrophobic. I wonder if you could just talk about that, especially in the south.

RK: One of my professors, J. C. Green, shocked me as an undergraduate. He said, "You're just an outsider. You just don't belong very well to anything." That's a weird insight from a person you don't know that well, but I think it's true, you know? Belonging in family, belonging in larger communities, just doesn't quite work. And I'm assuming that maybe we're a type? Maybe that's what being a writer is all about? Or maybe that's self-aggrandizing, and maybe it has nothing to do with being a writer. It was a lucky accident.

JAC: But you've been really close to your family, right? And I also think of family as being important to your fiction. So much of what you write about is family drama or the drama surrounding families. Or the various families that we create. Chosen family, for example. I mean, does family function in that way when you are writing? Are you writing a character who belongs, in part, to his/her family but never feels like he/she belongs?

RK: Well, yes. I mean, do I feel like a member of the Walton family? I never have. And the other word, I think, is loner: that one is more comfortable being alone. I think I gravitate more toward characters who feel that they want to belong. I feel more legitimate being in their skin, but I can appreciate that family dynamic. And I'm also not immune to the drama inherent in the family dynamic. The same as in the town and the church and all these other communities. The communities, if you look at them in the right way, they are the gifts that keep on giving.

JAC: So much of American drama is about that kitchen table realism—"mom is upstairs addicted to morphine; don't talk too loud." That kind of stuff. Did you ever want to become a playwright?

RK: Yes, when I went to Europe. It was like, "Go!"

JAC: Are there finished or unfinished plays out there?

RK: Well, most of them are juvenilia. But I have been writing on one. There's an essay by Horace Cayton; he wrote a book, and Louis Sinclair, who just won the Nobel Prize, the first American to win the Nobel Prize, wrote him a note congratulating him on it. He also put it in the novel. *Kingsblood Royal*. He was so impressed by this young black man. They started corresponding, and Louis invited him to his estate in Massachusetts, Thorvale Farm. And this young bourgeois black man from Seattle travels here to see the great man and found that he's this embittered, lonely, divorcé, among only the people he pays to take care of him, most of whom are black. And I just thought, "What a wonderful drama!" And I've tried it several times. But I haven't been able to crack the nut.

JAC: When was the last time you tried it?

RK: Well, I first tried this when I lived in New York, and I pulled it out a few times. Recently, I was looking for that essay.

JAC: There's Playmakers just over here. They would love to do an original Randall Kenan drama.

RK: Are you encouraging me?

JAC: I am. I love the work you do in fiction, but the talents you have in other places, for example, your essays. The collection *The Fire This Time* opens with this letter that you've written to your godson where you're trying to help him work through what it means to be a young African American in the twenty-first century. Is this something you feel, not just responsible to your godson for, but responsible to whoever, to articulate the difficulties of living in a black body in the south?

RK: Well, responsibility is a big word, but I think the impetus behind that whole thing was to articulate. It's become fashionable for black folk, especially black folk of a certain status, to talk about having *the talk* with their kids. I don't know; I think the killings last year brought that to the forefront. So, this has now become a rhetorical thing. "Well, I have to have that talk with my kid." And I think that essay was in '07,'06, whenever I wrote that. The idea of trying to itemize what that talk is composed of and trying to—and Du Bois talks about it, and I even talk about Du Bois in my book—have the veil lifted. Double consciousness. *Oh wow, I'm not one of them. I'm the other.* And making that clear to a young person—which I don't think comes from any one ceremony. I think it's an accumulation over time. But anyway, it's about lifting that veil. And the one thing I am proud of: I predict in that essay that people are going to stop using that term "diversity" and all these other bullshit terms and use the term "pluralism," which is what we're really talking about. And I've been hearing that word more.

JAC: There's a lot of predictive stuff in *Walking on Water* and thinking about race not as beyond. There's a lot in those essays that's predictive; they feel very prescient, very precocious, like you're predicting a lot of stuff.

RK: That's scary.

JAC: In your essays and fiction alike, you work through a lot of competing histories—personal history, communal history, regional history, national history—and how these histories get negotiated by you and your characters. How does one articulate or connect personal history to a larger history, whether that's your family's history, a region's history, a nation's history?

RK: I mean, that has always been where it's at for me. I get really frustrated with my students when their work is completely absent of history. These people exist on no plane. They have no preoccupations. They're working against nothing. They have nothing calling them. Bullshit! That's what people live. That's how you make characters. And I'm so interested in history. People get on me because I'll read about Danish history. I'll read about Japanese history. I'll read about the history of socialist women. It's all grist for the mill in a way, seeing how people work against understanding that. And history is the big story, just like I was talking about with *Cadmus and Harmony.* And really why I love that goddamn book so much is because this little Italian dude from Milan put together all the great mythology in one book. That kind of initiative appeals to me. He does it in such an elegant way. I think I reviewed it for *Spin Magazine,* and I said it reminded me of Sophia Loren throwing her boa up over her shoulder. Yeah. History motivates me.

JAC: A lot of times we think of magic, or the supernatural, or science fiction as existing sort of ahistorically. It's not *from* anywhere because this is a fantasy, but your fantasy is rooted in such specific history. I'm thinking of that last section of *Let the Dead Bury Their Dead*—all these fantastical things that are happening are rooted in a very specific historical moment for these characters.

RK: Well, yeah. It needs to be organic, and it needs to be logical. I mean it has to have story logic. I mean you can't just make some shit up just for the hell of it.

JAC: That's got to be the juvenilia writers, like *and then they . . .*

RK: *And then this happened* . . . yeah. And you can see that again with young writers. They haven't really thought about it. But I'm more interested in that—in the magic of mythology, in these gods or creatures [that] do things, with a purpose, and it comes out in their character.

JAC: Yeah, and it's a part of a history that we know and a history that we don't know. That's why we read stories: to learn the first one. Do you have a lot of students that turn in science fiction and fantasy?

RK: Yeah, but I don't find them approaching it in a very fresh way. They do it; they do it. Most of them are imitations of J. K. Rowling, which has really gotten me depressed. I mean, I like her the way I enjoy a fizzy summer drink. It's refreshing. It's fun. But it's not the good stuff. It doesn't get you high. Not the way you need to get high.

JAC: What are some of those science fiction or fantasy writers that do get you high?

RK: I still go back to Heinlein. I still think Bradbury's *Dandelion Wine* is just beautiful. Let's start there. And Bradbury, I think he was many different things. He was a very complicated man, Bradbury. Screenplays, he wrote a very good *Moby Dick* screenplay. But Bradbury also wrote some good science fiction, and his science fiction was more speculative and much more philosophical than even some of Isaac Asimov's was. But *Dandelion Wine, Something Wicked This Way Comes,* I think those two stick out. There might be other ones because there were so many books.

JAC: Did you grow up with *The Twilight Zone*?

RK: I did. And I'm sure you know about this new *Black Mirror.*

JAC: The Netflix series, right? Which sort of leads to me asking about popular culture in your fiction. Especially comic books. I mean, obviously comics were an outlet for imagination and reading, but why do they become so central to your fiction?

RK: There was a transgressive element, and the older I got and stuck with it, the more pushback I got from the adults around me. And, at one point, I was told I couldn't come into one relative's house with comic books. They were in my bag. She didn't know it. But, yeah, I think more those types of narratives in particular appealed to young adolescent boys. And this is where I will go back to that word "escape," which I usually shy away from because it has all sorts of valences and that sort of thing. But I think, especially for a black boy, (and I'm sure it's true for white boys too, and I don't mean to be too gender-specific about it, but I think women probably go to other venues), but I think for boys in particular the idea of escape in that way that the classical Stan Lee/DC universe created those guys who had secret identities. And then they were let out of themselves, and all this emotion and fury and power . . .

there was something basically appealing about that mythology. And it goes right back to Ovid. I mean it's an ancient sort of thing.

JAC: Yeah, that comic books are sort of the mythology of adolescents.

RK: And a very American type. I mean we look at those American mythologies, *Tall Tales, Paul Bunyan, Pecos Bill*. I mean that was all . . . it comes from the same river.

JAC: One of the things comic books do in a very strange way is to speak about race in a way that American popular culture usually ignores or dismisses. Racial identity in comic books is complicated. You mentioned *Black Panther*—there was *Luke Cage*—there were some figures that were specifically racialized at least.

RK: Brother Bootsie.

JAC: Some that were less complicated, but was that a reason that drew you?

RK: I mean, I think they were more successful when they metamorphized race than when they dealt with it head on. Luke Cage and Brother Bootsie, I just remembered, were huge failures, but I think when they came up with another metaphor for race (this was starting an historic trend?) I was talking to somebody about the black man in *Star Trek* and how we like to get away to *Star Trek* to get away from race. And Daniel Wallace said, "Damn Klingons." I think that's true of the Marvel universe as well, with the mutants. And I think Ryan Singer and all those writers, they read it so heavyhanded. There's a little more nuance with Chris Claremont and those guys.

JAC: You're someone who writes a lot about popular culture, and you're clearly a consumer—and your characters are consumers of it: they're aware of popular culture. How does popular culture operate for you in the stuff you write about?

RK: I mean, yeah, I think that's the real deal. People who don't consume popular culture are a little suspect in my world. If they can't talk about it, don't watch TV, don't keep up with news on any level. Actually, I just don't think they're interesting people, and they're certainly not people I'm interested in writing about. I think I had some characters—but they're not at the center of things.

JAC: I'm thinking of the character in "When We All Get to Heaven" who is so blissfully unaware of the fact that he's meeting this pop culture icon. And then he goes back to the hotel and sees the performer on the screen; there's this moment where he's watching him and realizing. And it's no big deal, right? That would be an example of a character who doesn't watch TV, doesn't keep up.

RK: He watches the Discovery Channel. He doesn't watch music videos. My sister watches a lot of TV, but when we're home and we turn on *The Walking*

*Dead,* she can't deal with it. "What is this crap? What's wrong with that man?"

JAC: We've talked a bit about the idea of an illusory world of [the] black middle class, what that supposedly offers to African Americans. In *The Fire This Time,* you write about the founder of *Ebony* and fantasies of accumulating wealth. The division of class is a real thing in communities and even more so than maybe racial differences, or maybe just because we don't talk about it as much. Could that be the thing?

RK: I think what Zora Neale Hurston used to call the Niggerati—among the Niggerati they used to talk about it a lot more. The book I bisect in that first chapter when I go to Martha's Vineyard, *Black Bourgeoisie* by E. Franklin Frasier, that book was hugely important decades after it was published, because it talked about something that got added. I think just like that brief book I mentioned by a literary scholar whose son I worked with, Paul Fussell, about class, which gives an x-ray of American class system. It's about the proletariat, the middle class. He's really an X-class, which always gave me hope. "Okay, I'm not in any of these people. I'm in ex class system, goddammit." I think there was a time when the whole idea that animated John H. Johnson and his wife, who was from this old-guard bourgeoisie, or the idea of Booker T. Washington, lifting one up by one's bootstraps, what a weird metaphor that is. He kind of tried to collide the two in a way that didn't work then and certainly is not going to work now. I think now that whole mythology has not been dismantled, it's just become dilapidated. It's like a decaying old mansion. There are still black cotillions in Savannah still, and there's probably one over in Raleigh. They were irrelevant, you know, largely in 1976. In 2016, they're almost figments of people's imagination. Anybody who still buys into that now, I can't see them fitting in anywhere in America. Not without medication.

JAC: In "Sorrow Songs," you talk about music and how you're trying to write a story of this actual thing that happened in Memphis. But you can't do it. It needs to be a song, blues especially. And your fiction is downright obsessed with music. Is there something about music that works a kind of magic that maybe fiction can't?

RK: Um, my classmate here, when I became a novelist, she was doing a residency at Providence, Rhode Island. We had this conversation, and she said, "Well, I'm like you. I really want to be a singer." And the feel of singing is that there is no confusion between the reader—I mean the singer—and the hearer, the listener, on what the emotion is. You know that exactly. But those squiggles on the page, you have to take into the computer. Translate. I think that's one of the appeals of music. You know exactly what they're feeling.

Sondheim can let you feel whatever he wants you to feel, whenever he wants you to feel it, in the way he wants you to feel it, for the amount of time he wants you to feel it.

JAC: Did you ever think about writing songs, or do you have any kind of facility with music or a skill set?

RK: I tried. As one of my friends said, "If you don't excel in something, it's because you don't want to put the time into it." It's a very hard, very Protestant way of looking at things. But, in the end, that's probably the truth. It wasn't that important to me.

JAC: A lot of your creative energy is spent articulating, not just, I think, cultural truths or truth about America, but I do think it's fair to say that you're interested in region. You have your postage stamp of "Tims Creek," the writing you did for *A Time Not Here,* this edited collection about North Carolina food: what is it about the south as a region, then? I know southern writers bristle whenever you talk about the south and their writing; I get that, especially in a homogenized or global culture. So, maybe it's a market? But I also do think there's something about region and especially this region that is compelling. What is that? For you?

RK: I don't think I take it as seriously as it may appear. I get invited to do a lot of these things. To me it's a very visceral thing, and it also has to do with the history. I wrote this piece recently because I had this very visceral response to a panel of all-white novelists talking about the south. And someone in the audience, after they had their talk, asked them about race. And the response was just . . . so I wrote about how you can't really talk about the south and deal with it honestly unless you deal with slavery and the history of slavery. So, I think when I'm talking about the south I'm talking about a different south than a lot of the academics are talking about. I mean, not all of them, but it's the *Gone with the Wind* bullshit. It's that kind of nostalgia and moonlight and magnolias.

JAC: White paternalism.

RK: Yeah.

JAC: Heteronormativity.

RK: Yeah.

JAC: Patriarchy.

RK: Yeah, so I'm more interested in uncovering the history of the Northwest Passage, you know? And also, when I talk to black kids about this, it's not a sad story. It's not just *Twelve Years a Slave*. God bless his heart—the guy who made that movie and all that. But the larger part is this triumphalism and the idea that you went through all this claptrap and you came out to be the First Lady of the United States. Because her people came from one of the most brutal rice plantations in North America. And the fact that you can go on to that is more inspiring and more interesting: it's why I don't let it go so lightly.

JAC: Staying with emotional and physical landscape for a second, you have traveled so much—I'm thinking not just about the work you did for *Walking on Water* but the fellowships you've had. You've been all over the world. How important is that to writing?

RK: For me, but I think you have to be that kind of person who's interested in it. I think it would be wasted on—I mean this sounds very judgmental, but it's true—it would be wasted on a lot of writers I know, writers who are so into their own navel. They can go from here to Timbuktu and not notice anything. I think you have to be the sort of person who is interested in the world, and if you are, you'll get out there anyway. You won't need me to tell you to do it.

JAC: When you were in Rome, for example, that was when you were finishing *Walking on Water,* which is, I think it would be fair to say, a heavily introspective book in the sense that it's mostly interested in one culture, American culture, and in exploring this one thing which is race. And here you were living abroad, internationally. Did this time writing it in Rome change, do you think, what you would have written if you were in Oxford, Mississippi, or if you were in Tuscaloosa, Alabama?

RK: That's an interesting question, because my knee-jerk response is, theoretically, no. Because I had done all the traveling—this was the idea, my vision of what that year was going to be. I'd done all the traveling. I'd had all the transcripts and reduced them somewhat. I had all my journals, which I was going to rewrite. And I was just going to hold myself in that beautiful palace, in my little room, eat good food, drink good wine, hang out with some good people, and do that. Which succeeded for the most part because what I had set out for myself was doable. But having that much in front of me, I didn't really get my mind around how much I had bitten off. I mean just technically. Going through all those transcripts, and then again I had set out for myself the task of doing it like Studs Terkel had done it—which means I didn't make up anything. And, unlike my hero, William Heat-Moon, I didn't just write what I wanted and send it to the person and say, *Is this okay, can we say you said this?* No, I didn't do all that, so I was very micro-involved.

JAC: Eating good food. What is it about food? You've got this published collection; there's so much about food in your words when we write emails. You have a lot of these quotes at the bottom of your emails. A lot of them are about food. What is it about food that is so haunting to you? It's more than just being a foodie, as you have been described.

RK: Well, I don't want to brag about it, but I will: John Egerton, who founded the Southern Foodways Alliance, his first book on southern food, which was called *Southern Food,* he excerpted a piece from an unpublished novel by an unpublished writer named RK. University of North Carolina Press has just republished it. And, yeah, the hog-killing scene [from *Visitation*]. He read that; his editor was my editor, the one who edited *Walking on Water.* Ann Post: I was working for her. I was her assistant. And I guess she said, *I think you'll like this manuscript*. She gave it to John. He was visiting and called me into his office one day and told me he was going do that. So, yeah, I've always been encouraged to write about food. I always did it naturally. A lot of those stories, *Let the Dead Bury Their Dead,* are full of food. And it's not as much in *Walking on Water,* but I really wanted to see how alive that was throughout the diaspora in North America. And the thing that failed there is that some of the people I picked weren't as interested in talking about food as others. Not that I didn't ask. But they'd say, *Hey, I only eat at McDonald's.* That doesn't make you not black, but that doesn't interest me.

JAC: Is there anything just off-limits to you? I'm not going to write about that—whether it's something that's too close or as a writer?

RK: I think I approach that point intuitively. I mean there are times when you have gone a bridge too far: that infamous speech that Lionel Schreiber gave in Australia this summer where she wore a sombrero and got up and talked about white privilege doesn't exist. There are some things where I would say I just ain't going there. And I know that it's a bridge too far, that I would have to do a lot more research and experience and interviewing people to dare get into it. And sometimes you bump up against it, and things come to me like mushrooms. You know, oh wow, that is a great story. And again, intuitively, I say, ooh, *better leave lay where Jesus wanted it*. Although, the more forbidding it seems, the more compelled I am, the more interesting, the more I know that there's something there. I mean that's the stuff people want.

JAC: In "Clarence and the Dead," do you have people uncomfortable with the intimacy between a man and a child?

RK: Well, I knew the suggestion of the liaison between the two was potent. I also knew it was absurd. The idea that this absurdity would go over your head or you would be ignorant enough to be offended by it, then I was doing my job.

JAC: At the end of *The Fire This Time,* there's this really great moment where you just start looking at a lot of major African American public figures, one of whom, of course, is Senator Barack Obama. And you talk about him as a kind of a raven, as a liminal figure, one that could potentially become transformative for African American culture. Did he become that for you? How do you read him?

RK: I look back at that now—I mean, maybe not enough time has passed, maybe too much time has passed—I don't know if I sold that metaphor the way I wanted to. I mean, taking from Joel Chandler Harris and the whole African structure of using animals as archetypes for people. I wonder now if it was the right metaphor. I also stole from Paul Fussell, the whole X-class thing. The ravens were my X-class, but I just have a feeling ravens comes off as being too aspirational and too hopey-changey? Which is named Barack Obama. But I believe in something like that, and David Brooks, in his book about class, *Bobos in Paradise,* comes up with a new class, bourgeois bohemians. They are a self-determined meritocracy, and the big bobo of our time is Oprah Winfrey. And I would put both Michelle and Barack in that bobo class, both in terms of their cultural taste and their financial freedom and all that sort of thing. But I think it's important to understand how I arrived there. I think, especially in this sound-bite era, to say it out of that context, without understanding Brer Rabbit and Brother Bear, and all that sort of thing, it might lose something. And then maybe I should have said "crow." Would that sound too Jim Crow? That's that connotation.

JAC: Race and American culture, especially political popular culture, feels at one time very dynamic, it's ever-changing, mutating, but also somewhat static in that we read race so uncomplicatedly and have for so long. Do you feel a book like *Walking on Water* needs a coda or something? After "Black Lives Matter," and "I Can't Breathe," and "Say Her Name," and all these other movements that are happening—not to mention the emerging Trumpism? Do you feel like *Walking on Water* is a cultural and historical artifact of the time when you articulated some truths about American whiteness that were true then that aren't true now? And so, those need some sort of reinvention, or rearticulation?

RK: When I first started doing it, I realized that it was probably going to be necessary and how fun it would be, you know, go back on the road twenty years later! Now I'm thinking *Hell, no*! But there was someone who inspired me, John A. Williams, a novelist I admire a great deal, *The Man Who Cried I Am*. He did a very elegant little book, and, compared to what I did, was really tiny for *Holiday Magazine*. It was called *This Is My Country Too,* and I even quote him from time to time. And I thought *I'll go to some of the same places he went to*. Some places there was no other reason to go there other than John A. Williams went here in 1962. My agent wanted me to find a physical metaphor, like the underground railroad. I'd been thinking about a book about cowboys, I probably mentioned that to you. I don't think that's going to be enough. I think I'd have to do something else. But, yeah, I do think it's going to need some translation.

JAC: Do you think you could get a book deal on a project like that now? I'm not talking about *you,* even: do you think a young African American writer could get a book deal like that now?

RK: I think with updating, with tweaks, I think the concept would work. There's a lot of lamentation right now about how the publishing world has become very constrictive and even quality work is having a hard time, and so you need to come with some sort of herald, some sort of imprimatur. Either you have fifty thousand Facebook friends or Twitter power, or you have some story that's going to break through. And, it's been seventeen years since that book came out? Race is still on people's lips, you know? And it's been handled so hamfistedly by so many people. So, to answer your question, yeah, I think it's possible.

JAC: Circling back around to our beginning: Are you, still now, conscious of yourself writing back not just to the people that you were writing to before but writing back to yourself, writing in the wake of successes and failures?

RK: I'm still writing back to those texts that I encountered. It's astonishing how foundational—I mean like pillars in one's life—those texts become. Maybe not for everybody, but for me. That's why that series I told you about, *Black Sails,* is so important: it's me coming back to *Treasure Island.* It's why I had this epiphany that *There's a Man Going 'Round Taking Names* is really a rewriting of *Treasure Island,* in a funky kind of way. I don't think it will be obvious—I was upset that it wasn't obvious that *Visitation of Spirits* was a rewriting of *A Christmas Carol.* Yeah, it's probably even funkier than that. And insofar as I'm talking to that boy who was reading those books, yes. I have some flashes when I'm writing the two young men in that novel. It's odd that in this novella that I'm going to turn in, *Resurrection Hardware,* his youth is kind of obscure. I mean, because it's short, about 120 pages. It's not something I'm obsessed with. I'm more obsessed with the sex, but that is a way of being in conversation with my youth.

JAC: Is it just you writing back to these same people that you're always writing to? I mean, maybe the conversation shifts, but it always starts from this desire to talk back to them?

RK: Well, I've been so fortunate, because I feel there are so many. I mean, I'm a poor boy from Chinquapin, North Carolina; when I say I had a really good education, I don't mean I was Winston Churchill or anything, you know? I wasn't studying Greek and Latin, but I was given some good books to read. Enough to last me the rest of my life.

# APPENDIX B

## *Tims Creek Genealogy*

**Tims Creek Chronicles**

*Cross Family (Black)*

ANNE GREENE—Wife to Pastor Jimmy Greene. Radical social worker who dies of ovarian cancer in her late 20s.

ARETHA "RETHA" CROSS—wife of Zeke, mother of Sammy, grandmother of Horace.

EZEKIEL "ZEKE" CROSS—Farmer, father of Samuel, husband of Retha, grandfather of Horace.

EZRA CROSS—Great-great-grandfather to Horace. Born enslaved on a Cross plantation, Charybdis, which will form the heart of Crosstown, county seat of York County. At one point owns a large swath of the swampland that will become Tims Creek.

FOUR DAUGHTERS OF JONNIE MAE GREENE: Rachel, Rebecca, Ruthester—All teachers educated at North Carolina Historical Black Colleges; Rose, mother of Jimmie, who left home as a teenager, and has lived abroad for most of her life. Mother to Isadore and Franklin as well as Jimmy.

HORACE CROSS—Rising senior at East York High School, outside Tims Creek, N.C. Dies by his own hand in the spring of 1985 under extraordinary circumstances.

JIMMY GREENE—Son of Rose, grandson of Jonnie Mae, pastor of First Baptist Church of Tims Creek. Successor to Hezekiah Barden.

JONNIE MAE GREENE, NEE CROSS—sister of Zeke, grandmother to Jimmy Greene.

LESTER CROSS—Son of Johnny Mae, father of Clara Cross DePriest.

RUTH CROSS NEE DAVIS—wife to Jethro, brother to Jonnie Mae and Zeke. A widow for more than sixty years. Lives to be a centenarian.

SAMUEL/SAM/SAMMY CROSS—Son of Zeke, father of Horace

THOMAS CROSS—Great-grandfather to Horace. Deacon of First Baptist of Tims Creek.

*Cross Family (White)*

ALEXANDER FISH, FISH OWEN ALEXANDER, AND PHINEAUS OWEN, who would go on to establish himself as a leading natural historian, focusing on the flora of North America, especially the American south. Alexander and Fish both serve the Confederacy during the Civil War while Phineaus is abroad. Oldest son, Owen Alexander, becomes estranged from his family, absconds with an enslaved woman of whom he is enamored and who he renames Clytemnestra, to the mountains of North Carolina. The family has him officially declared deceased and actively disowns any acknowledged children.

OWEN ALEXANDER CROSS—North Carolina magistrate, North Carolina state senator during mid-nineteenth century.

OWEN "BUCK" CROSS—Revolutionary War hero; traditionally considered founder of family in North America. First farm established outside of Wilmington, North Carolina, becomes Charybdis Plantation, the heart of the future Crosstown, North Carolina.

OWEN PHILLIP CROSS—Theologian, activist. Famously kidnapped at the age of ten by Marxist radicals in 1970. Also kidnaped: ten-year-old Jean-Luc dePreist of Chapel Hill.

OWEN PHINEAUS "O. P." CROSS—twentieth-century patriarch of North Carolina Cross family. Brother to Christina Anne Archer Cromwell, who married two captains of industry.

PATRICIA CROSS NEE TERRELL—wife of O. P. Cross, sister to Percy Terrell, granddaughter of Malcolm Terrell.

PHILIP CROSS—Youngest son of O. P. Cross and Patricia Cross. Father of Owen Phillip Cross.

REBECCA CROSS, NEE FISH—Wife to Senator Cross. Mother to four sons.

*Others*

AARON STREETER—D.C. attorney, son to Aaron, half-brother to Jamonica.

DR. AARON STREETER—transplanted Philadelphian, physician. Father to Aaron.

EDWARD WILLIAMS—Who dies in a car wreck outside Boston; lover to Gabriel.

Gideon Stone—Once teenage love to Horace Cross; becomes lover to Owen Phillip Cross. Graduate of Columbia Medical School.

Gloria Brown—Wife to Raymond Brown. Divorced. Mother to Tamara.

Hezekiah Barden—Pastor of First Baptist Church of Tims Creek. Successor to Jimmy Greene.

Ida Perry—Widow of the late Honorable "Butch" Perry. Lives in a house reputed to be haunted.

Jamonica Streeter—Lovechild of Aaron Streeter.

Lucious Stone—Local farmer. Infamously known as distiller and seller of illegal spirits. Father to Gideon, future physician.

Mabel Pearsall—Elementary school teacher and mother. Convicted of involuntary manslaughter of an infant. Received time served.

Maggie Williams—Proprietress of local Tims Creek hardware store founded by her late husband, Thomas. Grandmother to the late Edward Williams.

McElwaine Family—Descendants of Elihu Increase McElwaine, thought to have been a runaway slave originally from Mississippi. He becomes a prosperous lumberman and farmer, credited with draining much of what becomes the town of Tims Creek. Among his descendants are Tabitha and Elihu, who become confidantes of Booker T. Washington, and a great-great-great grandson, Elihu, who matriculates at the University of North Carolina at Chapel Hill in the mid-1960s and is reputed to have kidnapped both Owen Phillip Cross and Jean-Luc DePreist in 1970.

"Pharaoh"/Menes—Traditional founder of Tims Creek (originally named "Thames Creek" by Phineaus Cross in 1859). Yoruba leader; mutineer, slave ship *Jesus*.

Ray Brown—Funeral director, proprietor of the Raymond Brown Funeral Home, founded by his father and grandmother.

Tarrell Family—descendants of Malcolm Tarrell, lumber baron and local merchant in eastern York County. Father of Percy, who diversifies family holdings and who is an avid hunter. Father of Patricia, who weds into the Cross family of Chapel Hill.

Viola Honeyblue Stone—wife to Lucious; mother to Gideon.

# NOTES

**Chapter 1: Understanding Randall Kenan**

1. Randall Kenan, interview by James A. Crank, June 13, 2016, transcript from a personal interview with the author in Chapel Hill, North Carolina. My thanks to the CARSCA committee at the University of Alabama for funding my trip to Chapel Hill to interview Mr. Kenan.

2. Randall Kenan, "Brother Rabbit versus Brother Fox," in Kenan, *The Fire This Time* (Hoboken, N.J.: Melville House, 2007), 44.

3. Randall Kenan (Crank Interview).

4. Kenan, "Brother Rabbit versus Brother Fox," 44.

5. Ibid., 44.

6. Randall Kenan (Crank Interview).

7. Kenan, "Brother Rabbit versus Brother Fox," 44.

8. Randall Kenan, *Walking on Water: Black American Lives at the Turn of the Twenty-First Century* (New York: Knopf, 1999), 608.

9. Randall Kenan (Crank Interview). The remainder of the quoted material in this chapter comes directly from the Crank interview with Randall Kenan.

**Chapter 2: A Community of Ghosts**

1. Randall Kenan, *A Visitation of Spirits* (New York: Grove, 1989): back cover. Parenthetical citations in the remainder of this chapter come from this edition of Kenan's novel.

2. Trudier Harris, *The Scary Mason-Dixon Line: African American Writers and the South* (Athens: University of Georgia Press, 2009), 119.

3. Charles Rowell, Interview with Randall Kenan, Callaloo 21.1 (1999): 144–145.

4. Antiwan Walker, "Queering Black Nationalism: History, Geopolitics, and Sexual Identity in Randall Kenan's A Visitation of Spirits," CLA Journal 56.1 (September 2012): 54.

5. Robert McRuer, "A Visitation of Difference: Randall Kenan and Black Queer Theory," in *Critical Essays: Gay and Lesbian Writers of Color,* edited by Emmanuel Nelson (Binghampton, N.Y.: Haworth, 1993), 227.

6. Walker, "Queering Black Nationalism," 55.

7. Harry Thomas, "'A Wanderer on the Earth' and 'A Son of the Community,'" *North Carolina Literary Review* 17 (October 2008): 126.

8. Lindsey Tucker, "Gay Identity, Conjure, and the Uses of Postmodern Ethnography in the Fictions of Randall Kenan," *Modern Fiction Studies* 49.2 (Summer 2003): 313.

9. Harris, *The Scary Mason-Dixon Line,* 123.
10. V. Hunt, "A Conversation with Randall Kenan," *African American Review* 29:3 (Autumn 1995): 416.
11. Walker, "Queering Black Nationalism," 80.

**Chapter 3: Speaking for/Speaking to the Dead**

1. Randall Kenan, *Let the Dead Bury Their Dead* (New York: Harcourt Brace Jovanovich, 1992): front cover. Parenthetical citations in the remainder of this chapter come from this edition of Kenan's book.
2. Howard Frank Mosher, "The Ghost on Main Street," NYTimes.com, June 14, 1992, http://www.nytimes.com/1992/06/14/books/the-ghosts-on-main-street.html (accessed 12 March 2017).
3. Ibid.
4. V. Hunt, "A Conversation with Randall Kenan," *African American Review* 29:3 (Autumn 1995): 418.
5. Lindsey Tucker, "Gay Identity, Conjure, and the Uses of Postmodern Ethnography in the Fictions of Randall Kenan," *Modern Fiction Studies* 49.2 (Summer 2003): 306.
6. Hunt, "A Conversation with Randall Kenan," 416.
7. See Trudier Harris, "Southern Voices: Southern Tales, Randall Kenan's 'Clarence and the Dead,'" in *The Power of the Porch: The Storyteller's Craft in Zora Neale Hurston, Gloria Naylor, and Randall Kenan* (Athens: University of Georgia Press, 1996).
8. Hunt, "A Conversation with Randall Kenan," 414.
9. DiAnne Malone, "Interview with Randall Kenan," turnrow.ulm.edu, http://turnrow.ulm.edu/view.php?i=105&setcat=interview (accessed 12 March 2017).
10. Uzzie T. Cannon, "Disturbing the African American Community: Defamiliarization in Randall Kenan's Let the Dead Bury Their Dead," Southern Literary Journal 42.1 (Fall 2009): 107.
11. Ibid., 118.
12. Ibid., 102.

**Chapter 4: Brother Baldwin and the Shadow of Tims Creek**

1. Randall Kenan, "Sorrow's Child," *The Nation* 28 (December 1992): 815–816. Parenthetical citations in this section (until note 2) come from this publication.
2. Randall Kenan, *James Baldwin,* (New York: Chelsea House, 1994).
3. Norman Mauskop and Randall Kenan, *A Time Not Here: The Mississippi Delta* (Santa Fe, N.M.: Twin Palms, 1997).
4. Randall Kenan, "Now Why Come That Is?," *Callaloo* 21.1 (1998): 119–132. Parenthetical citations in this section (until note 5) come from this publication.
5. Randall Kenan, *Walking on Water: Black American Lives at the Turn of the Twenty-First Century* (New York: Knopf, 1999). Parenthetical citations in this section (until note 8) come from this publication.
6. V. Hunt, "A Conversation with Randall Kenan," *African American Review* 29:3 (Autumn 1995): 419.
7. George Hovis, "'I Contain Multitudes'": Randall Kenan's *Walking on Water* as Collective Autobiography," *Southern Literary Journal* 36.2, Nineteenth Century Southern Writers (Spring 2004): 104.

8. Randall Kenan, *The Fire This Time* (Hoboken: Melville House, 2007). Parenthetical citations in this section (until note 9) come from this publication.

9. Randall Kenan, ed., *The Cross of Redemption: Uncollected Writings* (New York: Pantheon, 2010). Parenthetical citations in this section (until note 10) come from this publication.

10. Randall Kenan, "Randall Kenan on *Ode to Billie Joe*," *Personal in My Memory: The South in Popular Film*, 33–34. Parenthetical citations in this section (until note 11) come from this publication.

11. Randall Kenan, "When We All Get to Heaven," Virginia Quarterly Review 89.2 (2013): 114–121. Parenthetical citations in this section (until note 12) come from this publication.

12. Randall Kenan, ed., *The Carolina Table: North Carolina Writers on Food* (Hillsborough, N.C.: Eno, 2016). Parenthetical citations in this section come from this publication.

# SELECTED BIBLIOGRAPHY


**Works by Randall Kenan**

NOVELS/COLLECTIONS

*The Carolina Table: North Carolina Writers on Food*. Randall Kenan, editor. Hillsborough, N.C.: Eno, 2016.

*The Cross of Redemption: Uncollected Writings*. New York: Pantheon, 2010.

*The Fire This Time*. Hoboken: Melville House, 2007.

*James Baldwin*. New York: Chelsea House, 1994.

*Let the Dead Bury Their Dead and Other Stories*. San Diego: Harcourt Brace Jovanovich, 1992.

*A Visitation of Spirits: A Novel*. New York: Grove Press, 1989.

*Walking on Water: Black American Lives at the Turn of the Twenty-First Century*. New York: Knopf, 1999.

ESSAYS/NONFICTION

"Randall Kenan on *Ode to Billie Joe*." *Personal in My Memory: The South in Popular Film*. (2011): 33–34.

"Sorrow's Child." *The Nation*. 28 December 1992: 815–816.

JOURNALISM

*A Time Not Here: The Mississippi Delta*. Santa Fe: Twin Palms, 1997.

SHORT STORIES

"Now Why Come That Is?" *Callaloo* 21.1 (1998): 119–132.

"When We All Get to Heaven." *Virginia Quarterly Review* 89.2 (2013): 114–121.

INTERVIEWS

Hunt, V. "A Conversation with Randall Kenan." *African American Review* 29:3 (Autumn 1995): 4n–20, 417, 419.

Malone, DiAnee. "Interview with Randall Kenan." *Turnrow* 6.1 (2009). turnrow.ulm.edu. http://turnrow.ulm.edu/view.php?i=105&setcat=interview.

Marchando, Tiara. "Interview with Randall Kenan." *Pine Manor College* (2010). http://www.pmc.edu/randall-kenan-interview.

Mills, Fetzer, Jr. Interview with Randall Kenan. *Salon Magazine* (2001). http://www.cnn.com/books/news/9903/11/randall.kenan.salon/index.html.

Rowell, Charles. Interview with Randall Kenan. *Callaloo* 21.1 (Winter 1998): 35.

Rowell, Charles. Interview with Randall Kenan. *Callaloo* 21.1 (1999): 133–148.

**Works about Randall Kenan**

BOOK-LENGTH

Betts, Doris. "Myth and Reality in Tims Creek." *Southern Writers at Century's End.* Lexington: University of Kentucky Press, 2015. 9–20.

Gambone, Philip. "Randall Kenan." *Travels in a Gay Nation: Portraits of LGBTQ Americans.* Madison: University of Wisconsin Press, 2010. 175–185.

Harris, Trudier. "Southern Voices, Southern Tales, Randall Kenan's 'Clarence and the Dead.'" *The Power of the Porch: The Storytellers' Craft in Zora Neale Hurston, Gloria Naylor, and Randall Kenan.* Athens: University of Georgia Press, 1996.

Hovis, George. "Randall Kenan, The Black Yeoman." *Vale of Humility: Plain Folk in Contemporary North Carolina Fiction.* Columbia: University of South Carolina Press, 2007. 226–269.

McKoy, Shelia Smith. "Rescuing the Black Homosexual Lambs: Randall Kenan and the Reconstruction of Southern Gay Masculinity." *Contemporary Black Men's Fiction and Drama.* Ed. Keith Clark. Champagne: University of Illinois Press, 2001. 15–36.

McRuer, Robert. "A Visitation of Difference: Randall Kenan and Black Queer Theory." *Critical Essays: Gay and Lesbian Writers of Color.* Ed. John Dececco. London: Routledge, 2013. 221–234.

Norman, Brian. "Death and Futurity in Randall Kenan's Reinvention of the Passing Narrative." *Lit: Literature Interpretation Theory* 23 (2012): 52–69.

ESSAYS

Cannon, Uzzie T. "Disturbing the African American Community: Defamiliarization in Randall Kenan's 'Let the Dead Bury Their Dead.'" *Southern Literary Journal* 1 (2009): 102.

Costello, Brannon. "Randall Kenan beyond the Final Frontier: Science Fiction, Superheroes, and the South in *A Visitation of Spirits.*" *Southern Literary Journal* 1 (2010): 125.

Hovis, George. "'I Contain Multitudes': Randall Kenan's *Walking on Water* as Collective Autobiography." *Southern Literary Journal* 36.2 (2004): 100–125.

Littler, Lucy R. "'The Implications of 'Chosenness': Unsettling the Exodus Narrative as a Model for Black Liberation in Randall Kenan's 'A Visitation Of Spirits.'" *Southern Literary Journal* 44.1 (2011): 37–55.

McMahand, Donnie. "Strange Bedfellows: Randall Kenan Talks Back to the Southern Renaissance." *Southern Literary Journal* 47.2 (2015): 36–54.

Roark, Chris. "Randall Kenan." *Contemporary African American Novelists: A Bio Bibliographical Critical Sourcebook.* Ed. Emmanuel S. Nelson. Westport, Conn.: Greenwood Press, 1999. 243–249.

Tettenborn, Eva. "'But What If I Can't Change?': Desire, Denial, and Melancholia in Randall Kenan's *A Visitation of Spirits.*" *Southern Literary Journal* 2 (2008): 249.

Tucker, Lindsey. "Gay Identity, Conjure, and the Uses of Postmodern Ethnography in the Fictions of Randall Kenan." *Project MUSE. MFS Modern Fiction Studies* 2 (2003): 306. Wester, Maisha. "Haunting and Haunted Queerness: Randall Kenan's Re-Inscription of Difference in *A Visitation of Spirits.*" *Project MUSE. Callaloo* 4 (2008): 1035.

REVIEWS

Benedict, Pinckney. "Angels, Demons, and Men." Review of *Let the Dead Bury Their Dead*, by Randall Kenan. *Chicago Tribune Books*. May 1992. http://articles.chicagotribune.com/1992-05-03/entertainment/9202090295_1_hogs-randall-kenan-dead.

"The Fire This Time." Review of *The Fire This Time*, by Randall Kenan. Melville House.

Garrett, George. "Debut of a Virtuoso: A Courageous, Innovative First Novel Redefines the Shape of Black Fiction." Review of *A Visitation of Spirits*. *Chicago Tribune*. August 1989.

Korelitz, Jean Hanff. "Randall Kenan: To Live and Die in Dixie." Review of *Let the Dead Bury Their Dead*, by Randall Kenan. *Washington Post*. June 1992. https://www.washingtonpost.com/archive/entertainment/books/1992/08/02/randall-kenan-to-live-and-die-in-dixie/6d81ab0c-7346-4a59-8bce-90f8f610ffe3/?utm_term=.4e74169490de.

"Let the Dead Bury Their Dead and Other Stories." Review of *Let the Dead Bury Their Dead*, by Randall Kenan. *Kirkus*. January 1992. https://www.kirkusreviews.com/book-reviews/randall-kenan/let-the-dead-bury-their-dead/.

Mosher, Howard Frank. "The Ghosts on Main Street." Review of *Let the Dead Bury Their Dead,* by Randall Kenan. *New York Times*. June 1992. http://www.nytimes.com/1992/06/14/books/the-ghosts-on-main-street.html.

Norton, Girault. "Randall Kenan's Use of Double Plots." Review of *Let the Dead Bury Their Dead*, by Randall Kenan. *Barely South Review*. January 2011. http://barelysouthreview.digitalodu.com/all-issues/january-2011/randall-kenan%E2%80%99s-use-of-double-plots/.

"Walking on Water: Black American Lives at the Turn of the Twenty-First Century." Review of *Walking on Water: Black American Lives at the Turn of the Twenty-First Century*, by Randall Kenan. *Kirkus*. February 1999.

# INDEX